Best Wishes —

Lester Maddox

SPEAKING OUT

The Autobiography of
LESTER GARFIELD MADDOX

SPEAKING OUT:

The Autobiography of

LESTER GARFIELD MADDOX

Doubleday & Company, Inc., Garden City, New York, 1975

Library of Congress Cataloging in Publication Data

Maddox, Lester, 1915–
    Speaking out: the autobiography of Lester Garfield
Maddox.

    Includes index.
    1. Maddox, Lester, 1915–   I. Title.
F291.3.M3A33   975.8′04′0924 [B]
ISBN 0-385-08956-2
Library of Congress Catalog Card Number 74–2521

Contents

SPEAKING OUT

The Autobiography of
LESTER GARFIELD MADDOX

Chapter 1

Atlanta—The Other Side of the Tracks

I was born in 1915, in the shadow of the steel mill where my father worked in Atlanta, and our family never quite got out from under that shadow—literally and figuratively—throughout the years my brothers and sisters and I were growing up. We lived in a section of the city known as Tech Flats, where Mom and Dad raised chickens and had milk cows and a vegetable garden to supplement the income from the mill.

I was the second son born to Flonnie and Dean Maddox, with two boys and three girls to follow. Ours was a large family, which seemed to be the rule rather than the exception in those days, especially at our economic and social level. As jobs went, Dad's was relatively good, although by the yardsticks of today we would likely have been declared borderline poverty. In the teens and twenties he made about forty dollars a week as a roll-turner, work which required a high degree of skill but little education. The hours were long—fifty-five hours was the standard week—and the work was hard and the demands of a home with nine mouths to feed never let up on him. When his shift at the mill was over he would come home and spend hours working on the chicken house or the cow barn or in the vegetable garden. As likely as not there would be a Model T Ford in the backyard that he would tinker with until someone came along and made him an acceptable offer.

Mouths to feed, though, meant hands to work, and there was little time for idleness. When the mill whistle blew my brothers and I were waiting at home to help Dad as soon as he arrived, and Dad never believed a child with good hearing had to be told twice what was expected of him. If a reminder was needed, it came in the form of an ever present bundle of hickory switches and a trip with Dad to the barn.

I made as many of these trips as my brothers and these occasions often made me think he was too strict. But as the passage of time softened the sting of the hickory, my feelings changed. The enforced discipline evolved into a strong self-discipline that has stood me in good stead through a great many trying times.

We had kinfolks in Forsyth County forty-odd miles north of Atlanta, and occasionally the whole family would pile into the current Model T and head northward. The drive could take as much as an entire day, depending on the number of flat tires, breakdowns, and boilovers. Among the standard equipment were plenty of tire patches, a galvanized pail, lanterns as a backup for the electric lights, and a can of pepper or box of cornmeal to pour into the radiator to slow the leaks. We had a thorough knowledge of the location of all creeks near the roadway and when the leaky radiator boiled over the boys would tear off into the underbrush with the pail.

One winter Dad, my older brother Howard, and I drove up to Forsyth County to pick up a calf Dad had bought. Being the younger of the two boys, I was relegated to the back seat coming home that night. The calf rode with me. Calves, unfortunately, make no practical distinction between the barnyard and the back seat of a Model T Ford, and that particular trip stands out as vividly in my memory today as the day it happened.

We moved many times during my youth. Dad had a deep streak of the trader in him and we were like neighborhood gypsies, moving from block to block, up and down Fourteenth Street, over to State Street, as Dad would make a down payment on a vacant lot, build a house, then sell the one we were living in and move to the new place. He always turned a nice profit, which helped provide for his family. These moves seldom took us farther then a quarter of a mile, always well within earshot of the mill whistle. As was the case with many of the "blue collar" areas of Atlanta, the neighborhood was integrated. When we lived on State Street, eight or ten black families were living around the corner on Crawford Place. The black children and the white children played together without strife—perhaps because we did so by choice and not by decree.

As the years went by and the family grew, the frequency with which Dad came home late from the mill on payday, weaving his way to the door, increased. Mom was not a domineering woman, but she was dead set against alcohol, and she tried in vain to turn him around. There was no scarcity of drinkers in Tech Flats, nor was there any shortage of bootleggers in those days of Prohibition to provide them with whisky. I think I sensed, even as a child, that Dad's alcoholism was rooted in the deep frustrations he must have felt. He had no formal schooling. His reading and writing were painful and laborious and he knew full well that he had reached the peak of his earning power as a roll-turner in the mill, and that even with all his moonlighting efforts, he would never be able to provide for his family as he would have liked. I suppose he had the misfortune of being a perfectionist without the means to carry it out.

The real spiritual strength of our family was in Mom. Her entire life, apart from her love of family, was in her love of God. Every Sunday she would get all the children dressed in their best clothes and off we would go to the North Atlanta Baptist Church on Tenth Street, more often than not without Dad. Through her strong belief and example we came to know and trust in the will of the Almighty. This was the bond which held our family together.

Like most people of little education who see how the lack of it has held them back, Mom and Dad put a high priority on the education of their children. But at a point early in life it seemed that my own formal schooling might not exceed Dad's by more than a year or two. I experienced difficulty in the first grade at Home Park Elementary School, but I managed to be promoted to the second grade. On my way to school one morning I tripped over my raincoat and struck my forehead a severe blow on the edge of a heavy iron foot wiper. Several stitches were required and my schoolwork seemed to worsen after this. Then a routine eye examination conducted at school revealed that I was extremely nearsighted, a condition which obviously would cause me a great deal of difficulty in my efforts to keep up with my classmates.

The school authorities recommended to Mom that I be put in a special school where children with particular problems holding them back in regular classes could receive the individual attention they needed. She took me to this school one day and when I saw the books with the large print I realized that this would set me apart as being different from the average kids I knew, and I pleaded with her to let me go back to Home Park. I promised I would try harder and do better. I had already been examined for glasses, and she talked to the school officials and it was decided that I could have another chance.

The following Saturday she took me downtown to Whitehall Street, where a man fitted my new glasses on me. It was just at dusk as we came out of the store, and I recall my amazement at what I beheld. Never having had normal vision before, I had no reason to think the blurred images I saw were not as they should be. Now the buildings, lights, signs, people, everything up and down the street, stood out with startling clarity.

The glasses helped, of course, but I continued on through Home Park Elementary with no great scholastic distinction. During my final year there Mom became afflicted with a goiter and almost died. I had to quit school for several weeks to help out at home, washing diapers, doing housework, and even some of the cooking. I wanted to surprise the family at supper one night by serving them a three-layer chocolate cake. It was not bad considering it was my first effort, and the yellow specks in the icing were explained by the fact that the recipe had called for "eggs," not "whites of eggs."

Mom's health gradually improved. Ours was a neighborhood in the real sense of the word, and with our friends and neighbors helping out at home I was able to go back to Home Park and graduate. I wanted an education, and I went on to high school that fall. But I was also interested in business ventures, and making money. During this time our home was actually a miniature farming operation, with milk cows, a crop of vegetables, several hogs, and a flock of chickens. When our broilers were ready for market I would tie half a dozen of them together, sling them across my shoulder, and take them door to door around my neighborhood. When the lady of the house responded to my knock, I would give her a big grin and say: "Yes ma'am! I've got six of the finest fryers that were ever grown and I'm gonna sell all six of 'em to you for one dollar and twenty cents! That's right, just twenty cents apiece for these fine—"

As often as not I would get a broom waved at me and something like: "Run along, skinny! We got a yard full of them things our-selves!"

When our chickens and vegetables were ready, so were every-body else's. For me, the chicken business was better some years later, when I stopped trying to sell live birds and sold it skillet-fried.

In the summer I did as thousands of other youngsters have done and opened a soft drink stand at the curb in front of our house. If business got slow, I turned the stand over to my younger brother, Wesley, and walked several miles to Piedmont Park, where there was a nine-hole public golf course, and caddies were paid thirty-five cents a round. Ever since I had gotten fitted with glasses I had been reluctant to wear them except when absolutely necessary. Boys wearing glasses, for some reason, were looked on as being a bit on the sissy side. I never wore them when I caddied, with the result that I seldom saw where my employer's ball landed after he hit it.

One hot afternoon in July I arrived at the course looking for work. I offered my services to several golfers. I met with no suc-cess and started walking home. As I reached the tee of the second hole a man was preparing to hit his ball.

"Mister," I said, "I'll caddie the rest of the way for you for only a quarter."

He wiped at the perspiration on his forehead. "Okay, son, it's a deal. Here, take the bag and move down the fairway so you can watch where my drive goes."

I did as he told me and when I was about thirty yards ahead I lowered the bag and turned to watch. He teed the ball up, wag-gled his club a couple of times, and took a mighty swing, and a white blur streaked off the tee.

"Fore!" the man yelled.

By the time I saw the ball it was too late to get out of the way. It caromed off my head and I fell to the ground in pain. The next thing I was even vaguely aware of was the man's face swimming above me as he dabbed at my head with his handkerchief.

"You okay, son? My gosh! Why didn't you duck when I yelled!"

I tried to get up but everything kept swirling around me. The man helped me to my feet.

"We're getting you to the hospital, boy. That's a bad lick!"

I have a foggy recollection of an automobile ride, people gathering around me in a room, an X-ray machine, and then a day and a half recuperating in Grady Hospital. I had stitches, how many I don't know, and a headache that lasted a week or more.

But the man did pay me the quarter, and I chalked up caddying as one business from which I was retired.

Once when the circus came to town I got a job bagging peanuts, at three cents an hour. Peanuts sold very well and I immediately realized that bagging them for someone else for three cents an hour was the wrong end of the business to be in. I found a place in downtown Atlanta where I could buy parched peanuts for three cents a bag and I bought a couple of dozen bags and sold them on the streets for a nickel. This was better, but there was still some of the profit that I was not getting for my efforts. I did not see anything difficult about parching them, and so I went to the produce market (which was located beneath the downtown viaducts in what is now known as Underground Atlanta) and bought a supply of raw peanuts, purchased a hundred small brown paper bags, and walked the two and a half miles home to prepare my stock in trade. Mom cooked on a wood stove, and I had to chop wood, build a fire, parch and pack the peanuts, and walk the two and a half miles back downtown and sell them the next day. The extra effort netted me a dollar and a half for a fifty-cent investment, provided I did not burn or eat my stock.

I was not more than ten years old at the time, but I was already fascinated with private enterprise and the opportunities it afforded, and was already beginning to formulate my goal of becoming a businessman.

In the late 1920s I applied for a newspaper route with both the Atlanta *Constitution* and Atlanta *Journal,* and was turned down by both. There was another competitor at that time, the Hearst Atlanta *Georgian-American,* and I was given a route that no one else seemed to want. The reason no one wanted it was because there were only nineteen subscribers on the route encompassing much of Hemphill Avenue, Tenth Street, State Street, and Fourteenth Street, which covered some three miles. The nineteen subscribers had to be served seven days a week, rain or shine. The newsboy bought the papers for nine cents a week and sold them for fifteen, or a profit of six cents per subscriber.

If I had looked on it as merely walking twenty-one miles a week with a load of newspapers to make $1.14, I certainly would not have considered it. It could only be profitable if I built up the list of subscribers. In that neighborhood it was a simple economic fact that one newspaper was all most people could afford. If a family was taking the *Journal* the only way to sell them the *Georgian-American* was to get them to drop the *Journal,* or the morning Atlanta *Constitution.* I stopped at every house along the route, selling my paper, and after seven or eight weeks of hard work I had built the route from nineteen customers to seventy-nine, which brought on a proportionate drop in subscriptions of the competition.

It was not long before the sales representative for the other papers came around to see me. "I've got good news for you, Lester," he said. "Remember when you asked me about a paper route and I didn't have one? Well, I've got one now and it's right here in your neighborhood! Whatdya think of that?!"

"I'm sorry, sir," I replied, "but I'm not looking for a route now. I've got one and I'm doing pretty well with it."

After trying to convince me I would be better off with his papers and meeting with no success, he gave up and left. Many years later and even to the present, seeing the abuse the *Journal* and *Constitution* heaped upon me, I could only wonder if they might not be harboring a grudge.

When we were living on Fourteenth Street in 1929, one of the major rubber companies decided to build a plant in Atlanta and our house was part of the acreage that was quietly bought up. Dad signed a contract for $5,000, but when he found out what was taking place he realized he had been misled into selling too cheaply. He initiated legal action against the company and rather than go to court they agreed to let him keep the house, which Dad moved to a lot on State Street. After the house was moved Mom and Dad decided it was time for the Maddoxes to move up in the world, and the $5,000 was invested in a new Model A Ford and a down payment on a house on Collier Road. The State Street house was rented out and we moved out of the neighborhood for the first and only time. Compared to the other houses we had lived in the one on Collier Road was a palace.

But it was not to be. The country was suddenly plunged into the Depression, and as if this were not enough, Dad's drinking problem grew worse. He had difficulty in keeping full employment at the mill, and he felt that younger and less experienced roll-turners were being given preferential treatment over him. This combination eventually led to Dad getting into a fight with the mill superintendent, and Dad was fired.

Abruptly, from our new high the family found itself in the most trying of times. The loss of the job was extremely critical for Dad, for he was a one-trade man and there were no other steel mills in Georgia. He was suddenly without an income, a family of nine to support, house notes to pay, with no hope of finding an adequate job amid the millions of more adaptable men who were being laid off all over America.

The Depression struck everyone, including the tenants on State Street, and as they moved out, we moved back in. Dad found brief employment hauling blocks and bricks, and then a night job as a laborer at Link Belt Company for ten dollars a week, only to lose that when the company had to cut back. For a short while he worked in a foundry for nine dollars a week. The tragedy of his alcoholism now was that out of the meager funds he somehow managed to allocate a considerable portion to whisky.

Unable to find any kind of work, Mom and Dad bought several used washing machines for five or ten dollars apiece and took in laundry. One of the things Dad still clung to was the Model A Ford, and he used this for deliveries to the few customers he and Mom had, and for a commercial laundry.

I was going to Tech High School at that time. Often I would have no lunch. My shoes were worn out and patched and I had no socks. Instead of going to school many mornings when I left home I would walk miles out Ponce de Leon Avenue, or down Spring Street to downtown Atlanta, picking up a few cents here sweeping out a store, or a nickel there making a delivery. As luck would have it, I ran squarely into Dad one morning on Spring Street.

"What are you doing, son?" he said. "You're supposed to be in school."

I could not bring myself to tell him the real reason and I simply shrugged and said, "Just playing hooky, Dad."

"You know I've always tried to tell you how important an education is, Lester. I've got to punish you for doing this."

"Yes, sir, I know."

"Get in the car."

We drove home in silence, some of the laundry still undelivered in the back of the car. When we got to State Street he stopped and we walked into the house and to the customary place for punishment, the bathroom. I assumed the position and glanced back apprehensively as Dad picked up the bundle of hickory switches. I closed my eyes tightly, already feeling the sting. I waited, and when a few moments had passed without the blow falling, I opened my eyes again and looked around. Dad stood there, his face slack and expressionless, the switches hanging limply in his hand. I saw the muscle in his jaw twitch and then he put the bundle of hickory switches back in the corner and turned and walked out.

I did not entirely understand what had happened at the time, although I did later. Standing there ready to inflict my punishment he saw the futility of punishing me for trying to do what he had to do; to earn money for the support of the family.

With the unrelenting pressures on the family there was no way for all of us to continue in school. My older brother, Howard, was badly injured when a can of gasoline exploded in his hands, and it was up to me to pitch in for the support of the others. In the tenth grade I dropped out of school to go to work. I found a job as a delivery boy for a wholesale jeweler in downtown Atlanta, and worked a ten-hour day, six days a week, for a salary of four dollars. I thought I was bettering my lot when I found an opening at a pharmacy on Sixth Street, making deliveries, working the soda fountain, and general flunky. The salary was the same, but the hours were longer, even though the job had more variety. The good fortune was short-lived, however. The owner had been shot in a holdup a few weeks before I came to work for him, and his condition and the Depression soon caused him to close the store. Unable to pay me for the final week, he gave me the delivery bicycle and wished me well.

My next position brought with it a raise of nearly 15 per cent

. . . from four dollars to four-fifty. A dentist, Dr. Dean Chandler, hired me as an apprentice dental technician. In this capacity I worked under the supervision of a black man, who introduced me to the "bug," as the illegal lottery has long been called in Atlanta. Noticing the regular appearance of a man at the lab each morning, I asked my supervisor who he was.

"That's the bug man, Lester. You pick three numbers and you make a bet with him. If they're the same three numbers on the stock market page in the afternoon paper, then you win."

"How much do you win?"

"If you bet a penny, you win five dollars."

More than a week's salary for a penny! Five hundred to one! Then I began to think about it; you had a choice of 000 to 999, or a thousand numbers. The odds *against* winning were twice what you were paid if you won. Of all the money collected by the "bug," only half was paid out to the winners. I became convinced then, just as I am today, that there is absolutely no way an illegal operation of this sort can operate without the protection of the city authorities.

Dad's drinking had become steadily worse. He bought a small building and put it on the lot next door to our house, where he operated a store selling bread, light groceries, and a few other items. But the business did not fare well due to his drinking and his insulting of customers. It was up to me to find a better paying job. One day a friend told me that he was leaving the job he had and enrolling at Georgia Tech. "It's not a bad job, Lester, if you want to look into it. It's operating a stamping machine at Atlantic Steel, and it pays ten dollars a week."

"That's more than twice what I'm making now!"

"Go talk to Mr. Schukraft. He's my supervisor."

I knew Edgar Schukraft. He had been a friend of Dad's at the mill, although they had been in different departments. My first thought was of how Dad would feel about my seeking work at the place where he had been fired. But the family need was great, and I decided to go without telling him.

I was received warmly by Mr. Schukraft, and after talking for a while he told me the job was still open and it was mine if I wanted it. It was not necessary for him to repeat the offer. I was now making *twenty-five cents* an hour, and working a forty-hour week, thanks to the new minimum wage laws enacted by the Franklin Roosevelt administration. Not only were Mom and my brothers and sisters excited about my new job, but Dad was extremely pleased. His misfortune had borne no relation to Edgar Schukraft, and he had no false pride about one of his sons having to help carry the load.

Half my salary each week went to Mom for the household. Four dollars went into the bank, and the remaining dollar was relegated to the unprecedented luxury of pocket money, out of which I bought new shirts (fifty-nine cents each), pants (sixty-nine cents), and a Coke from time to time.

I was eighteen years old, my formal schooling behind me, and all outward appearances indicated that I was following in my father's footsteps. I loved my father, but I had seen what his life was like and the depths that his frustrations had driven him to, and I did not want to repeat it. The money I put in the bank represented my chance to escape that destiny. Since early childhood I had been fascinated by business. I had seen men standing in the doorways of their stores and shops, and I had seen the contentment and pride and accomplishment reflected in their faces. That was what I wanted, to stand in my own doorway, to plant my feet firmly on just one small piece of God's great earth and to know in my heart that this was mine to do with as I saw fit. I never had any question but what America was *the* land of opportunity, that regardless of your origins, you could make it by initiative, hard work, and faith in the Almighty. I had my goal, I had initiative, and hard work never scared me. Now, with God's help, I was on my way.

Chapter 2

Lester's Grill and Other Adventures

One day in the summer of 1933, not long after I had dropped out of school, I was walking down McMillan Street when I saw a pretty girl with dark brown hair and blue eyes sitting on her bicycle outside a little ice cream parlor. She was a stranger in the neighborhood and I said to myself, "She's the one for me!"

She finished the cone she was eating and without taking any notice of me she pedaled away. I asked the other kids about her and they said her name was Virginia Cox, and that her family had just moved into the neighborhood.

I had to meet Virginia Cox. I went out of my way to walk down the street she lived on in hopes of happening into her. I was operating my little store on State Street. This was the same store (twelve feet square) that Dad had tried to operate as a grocery and failed. I had reopened it with four dollars' worth of soft drinks and penny candy. One day, to my surprise, several girls stopped outside on their bicycles, and Virginia was among them. One of the other girls introduced us.

"That's a nice bike, Virginia," I said. "How about letting me take a ride?"

She smiled and got off. "All right, Lester."

This was my chance to make a big impression, so instead of getting on the seat I turned around, sat on the handlebars, and pedaled off riding backwards. I made it to the foot of the hill, started to make my turn in the street, and suddenly lost my balance, the bike going one way and Lester the other, landing painfully on the back of my head on the pavement.

After this inauspicious beginning, Virginia and I began to date, attending church services together at Center Street Methodist, visiting friends around the neighborhood, or going to the movies when I had the money. I was soon hopelessly in love, and about a year after meeting her, when I had taken the job at the steel mill, I proposed to Virginia Cox.

Virginia, being level-headed and practical, turned me down.

"I want to marry you, Lester," she said. "But we can't afford to do it yet." She looked at me for a moment and smiled. "I think we could get married when you're making a foreman's pay, that is, if you still want to."

Of course I wanted to! But a foreman made $33.50 a week and I was making only $12.50. It seemed impossible. But it did set me a goal, an important one. "All right, Virginia," I said. "It's agreed! And you'll see, it won't be long!"

Not long after starting at Atlantic Steel, I had learned a valuable lesson about long-range planning. One of the federal programs during the Depression was the WPA—Works Progress Administration—and in my desire for quick advancement I mistook a pay increase offered by WPA to be greener pastures, and I quit the mill and went on the government payroll. My mistake was immediately evident. It was outdoor work, and when it rained there was no work, consequently, no pay. It rained the first two days, and I hurried back to Mr. Schukraft, hoping my job had not been filled. Fortunately for me, it had not, and he took me back.

In 1935 the company opened a new operation, the Hoop Mill Galvanizing Plant, and Mr. Schukraft moved me into this plant as assistant foreman, at sixteen dollars a week. I went about my work with vigor and determination and moved up steadily in responsibility, if not proportionately in pay. Thus, at the early age of nineteen, I had been entrusted with the responsibility of hiring and firing, scheduling employees, shifts, days of operation, shipping, as well as setting prices to be charged to our customers. In addition to this, I worked with Dr. Sandelin, the company's chief metallurgist and a former Georgia Tech professor, on a metallurgical project, and did considerable research in steel and iron processing and finishing.

The broad experience proved invaluable in later years, along with the practical education I acquired in the workings of capitalism, economics, industry, and private enterprise. The pay was low, but the experience was invaluable, not to be found in books or schools at any price.

By the early spring of 1936 my salary had reached $19.75 a week, a figure I was proud of but which was a long way from the $33.50 goal Virginia and I had set. However, I decided—and Virginia agreed—the future held enough promise for us to go ahead with the wedding. We were married on May 9, 1936, in a preacher's home in Marietta.

Edgar Schukraft was very active in local politics, and my first real interest in political matters came about through him. During one particularly heated county election he asked me how I felt about the race.

"I haven't kept up with it," I told him.

"That's wrong, Lester," he admonished me. "You've got a responsibility as a citizen to concern yourself with politics. If you don't, you certainly can't complain when a politician takes advantage of you."

"What's one vote?"

He laughed. "If everybody said that, there wouldn't be *any* votes!" He glanced at his watch. "What are you doing tonight? How'd you like to go to a rally with me and hear what these fellows have to say?"

I had never attended a political rally, and I agreed to go with him.

It was held in a building on Tenth Street, and my recollection is that it was either the sheriff's or county commissioner's race. After that I went to several others and it was not long before I found myself fascinated by the political processes. I listened to what the candidates promised and later, when they were in office, I compared the promises with what they delivered, and the more I saw how these promises were ignored after election, the more disgusted I became. A candidate might run on a reform platform, promising to rid the community of illegal gambling and whisky, yet once he was in office the "bug" would operate as openly as before, and non-taxpaid whisky would flow as freely as ever. Like most working men, however, I could only decry situations like this and hope to find a better man the next time I entered the voting booth.

Virginia and I lived with her parents for a few months because of finances and then we moved into a little duplex on Home Park Avenue, and later to a larger place on Center Street, where—as my Dad had done before me—I raised chickens to supplement my income from the mill.

Of course, I was young and determined to work my way up and out and into business for myself. Yet things were so tightly budgeted that when I lost my $19.75 weekly pay walking home from the mill one Friday, it took us months to recover from the loss, even having to seek help from any of our relatives who could provide it.

I made the mistake of trying to recoup my loss by risking a few dollars at a little street carnival where there was a cash prize if you knocked down the stacked milk bottles with a ball. This ill-advised effort cost me several more precious dollars.

While we were living in the duplex on Home Park, our first child, Linda Sue, was born. Virginia, unfortunately, developed a kidney infection after this that was so serious as to keep her in bed for quite some time. I was night foreman at the galvanizing plant, and when I got home I had a full day's work keeping house and taking care of Virginia and the baby. It was a matter of months before Virginia was up and around and in relatively good health. Through all our problems we both maintained an unshakable faith in the future, and that, with our faith in God, saw us through times such as these.

Edgar Schukraft and I had our first serious conflict at the mill over my efforts to get a raise for a very deserving man who worked under me. As an example of how tough the mill policy regarding pay was, the raise I was striving for was five cents an hour. We were going to lose the man to another department where he could move up, and Mr. Schukraft and I were eyeball to eyeball over the matter of leaving the fellow at thirty-seven cents an hour, or raising him to forty-two. Finally, Mr. Schukraft glared at me. "This is no gold mine down here, Maddox!"

I leaned a little closer, jutting my chin out. "I sure know that! If it was, I would have got mine and been gone by now!"

Conditions at the mill, as in many other industries, were highly

1. An early family photograph. That's me on the left, with
sister Bethelyn and brother Howard.

2. This photograph of me was taken in 1940, while I was working as foreman at Atlantic Steel for $30 a week.

3. The opening of the Pickrick was a happy event for me and my wife, Virginia, and a lot of people came to celebrate it with us. (Photo by Kirk Wooster)

4. I like to chat with my employees before the restaurant opens for the day. (Photo courtesy Wide World Photos)

5. This monument was built "in memory of private property rights" after federal authorities stopped my fight for private enterprise and private property rights in September 1964 by forcing the closing of the Pickrick. (Photo courtesy Wide World Photos)

conducive to unionization. Not only was the pay low, but men were afraid to take time off even if they were sick, and reluctant to pause too often during work for a drink of water or a call of nature. The CIO made an attempt in the early forties which, not unexpectedly, met with strong company opposition. Employees who were found—or even suspected of—associating with union organizers stood in imminent danger of losing their jobs. This brought a final confrontation between me and management when two men who worked under me were reportedly seen riding in a car with a union man. I was told to fire the men. I responded by saying I could not do that, as they were two of the best workers I had.

"Put it on your report that you're cutting down on your force," I was told.

"How can I do that? We started a third shift just yesterday."

"Then say they're no good! That they're not doing the work!"

"I can't lie about them," I said flatly.

"How you do it is up to you. But *get rid of those two men!*" There was a pause. "Do as I tell you, Maddox, or you won't be working here yourself. Is that clear?"

"If I'm forced to lie to carry out my orders, then I have no choice but to leave. If those men are fired, somebody else will have to do it."

As important as my job was to me and my family, I had to quit.

Oddly, the two men whose actions had precipitated the incident stayed on, as the matter had become so widely known that the company could not afford to make martyrs of them. They were still there years later when I visited the mill.

I had to take the side I believed was right, and while private enterprise may be the engine that makes America move, the worker in a sense is the fuel that fires the engine and there is justification in bonding together when it becomes apparent that the industry places little or no value on human life. I could not tolerate industry taking advantage of the wage earner any more than I can abide the opposite.

Our second daughter, Ginny, had been born before I left the steel mill. I came home one night from a meeting at the Masonic Lodge to find Virginia ready to go to the hospital, where the baby was born minutes after we arrived. Now, with a wife and two children, and no savings in the bank, I had to get work and get it in a hurry. With no other steel mills in Georgia and all my practical experience in steel, I went to Bessemer, Alabama, and took a job at the Bessemer Galvanizing Works, a subsidiary of Nashville Bridge Company, at eighty-four cents an hour, the most money I had ever made.

Virginia was still in poor health and not at all up to moving to Alabama, and she and the children remained in Atlanta. I rented a room in a boarding house for myself and commuted back and forth on weekends in an old Model A Ford to be with my family.

It was not long after I took the job that the Japanese attacked Pearl Harbor, plunging America into the bloody World War. The need for steel immediately increased under the urgencies of wartime, and one day during that black December I came close to being a casualty myself. I was supervising the unloading of ship plates out of a gondola car. A huge overhead crane was lifting a load of about 10,000 pounds from the car when I saw the chains had not been attached properly to the load, and were slipping loose. It was almost instantaneous; I cried out a warning to the workers and turned quickly to escape whatever might come my way, but I was not nearly quick enough. One end of the heavy chain, with the massive forged hook, suddenly free of the weight it had been lifting, swung directly at me. It struck me violently in the back, lifting me out of the car and across to the concrete dock. My arm struck the pavement first with great force, driving the bones of my hand up through my wrist.

I was hospitalized for two weeks, during which time the doctors had to break the bones in order to pull those of my hand and fingers out of the wrist and arm and put them back in their proper order. It was more than two years before I could operate the fingers well enough to pick up an empty soft drink bottle.

Because of the growing needs of the family, I took additional work as an inspector of engineering materials with the Navy Department at the nearby Ingals Iron Works. I found a suitable place in Birmingham, a duplex, and Virginia and the children joined me.

Although she had been born in Birmingham, Virginia's ties were in Atlanta, and we were determined to move back there. As soon as I was assured by the Navy that my work as an inspector would be in the Atlanta area, I resigned at Bessemer, went full time with the Navy, and the Maddox family returned to Georgia.

There was a shortage of qualified inspectors of engineering materials, just as there were shortages in many other areas critical to the war effort, and I found myself traveling more and more as the months went by, traveling to defense plants all over the South. This created a problem at home, as Virginia had not regained her health and I felt my first duty was the welfare of my family.

When I found that there was no way to avoid extensive traveling, I weighed the alternatives, found a job as a salesman on a laundry route as a temporary measure, and quit the Navy job as they had not fulfilled the assurance about not having to travel.

Bell Aircraft was tooling up in a huge new plant in nearby Marietta, to build the B-29 Super Fortress, and I applied for work, went to Buffalo, New York, for a period of training, and came back to work in production control. Although I had been forced to leave high school before graduating, I had taken several correspondence courses in accounting and engineering over the years since, and I found the satisfaction of making a real contribution to America's war effort in my work at the bomber plant. I taught those under me the reading of blueprints, and when certain key parts were in short supply, improvised the manufacture of them in the plant. My self-education and the years in production at the steel mill were paying off.

Disaster almost struck us that year. I received an urgent call at the plant telling me that there was a fire at my home. The fire trucks were still there when I rushed home, but the blaze was out. Only one room had been badly damaged, although there was considerable loss of clothing, furniture, and smoke and water damage to other parts of the house.

I found Virginia and the children at a neighbor's home. She told me she had been taking a bath, and little Linda had been playing with a toy broom, which she poked into the fireplace. When the broom began to burn, the child quickly put it back into her box of toys so Mama would not find out. Luckily Virginia discovered it before the fire got completely out of control, and we had adequate insurance coverage on the damage to clothing and other personal belongings so that the financial loss was minimal. It brought to mind a similar incident that happened to me when I was two or three years old. Having seen Mom and Dad put newspapers in the fireplace, I stuffed an unused bathroom heater with them and caught the room on fire. The fire trucks came quickly and the damage to the house was not serious. The damage to my backside was sufficient to teach me a very good lesson about fire, nevertheless.

I was doing well at my job, making about eighty dollars a week, getting in overtime in the nation's urgency to turn the tide of the war. By the time the first fifteen planes had rolled off the line, however, things seemed to change. Poor planning caused parts shortages, often shutting down the line. Workers stood idle, waiting and watching the clock for time to punch out. I was one of many required to come in on Sundays, at time and a half, and have nothing to do. I was completely frustrated, willing to work, wanting to work, and having little or nothing to do.

The waste in manpower and material grew to outrageous proportions, and the reason was distressingly obvious: the contracts with the government were cost-plus, which is perhaps the greatest encouragement to inefficiency that has ever been devised. The bigger the cost, the bigger the profit.

Seeing hundreds of people standing about idly while drawing overtime, I knew that I could no longer participate in it. I mailed my ID badge to Bell Aircraft one day and never went back.

I decided now was the time to go into business for myself, even though our life savings were $400, not the $1,000 I had set as my goal. I bought a small business at the corner of Fourteenth and State streets, in the heart of the old neighborhood, for a down payment of $100. I sold the chickens we raised in our backyard, tore down the chicken house for the materials in it, and by the time I had finished expansion the building measured about twenty-two by ten feet. I had built a counter with four stools, a pair of drugstore style tables with four chairs each, a grill, refrigerator, freezer, but no hot water or rest room facilities. My stock consisted of ice cream, sandwich makings, soft drinks, rat poison, work gloves, candy, razor blades, and numerous other sundries and notions. Lester's Grill opened to something less than a stampede of customers.

It supplied a need in the neighborhood, however, and business grew. I was soon making enough money to support the family— now grown to five with the arrival of Lester, Jr.—if not in style, at least with the necessities.

My leaving the bomber plant called for a trip to the draft board, where it was pointed out that I had left a war job.

"It may be a war plant, sir," I responded, "but it wasn't a war job."

"Someone had to be hired to replace you," the interviewer said.

"Not for the work I did," I replied honestly. "They may very well have another man on the payroll, but he's not there to replace me for the work I was doing, because they didn't give me anything to do!"

I was given a physical exam and classified with a hardship deferment because of Virginia's chronic ill health.

Lester's Grill continued to be a successful operation, so much so that less than a year after I opened, I had an offer of $4,000 for the business. Since there was no way it could grow, I decided to take the offer, and while waiting to close the sale I found a grocery store at the corner of Hampton and Eighth that was for sale. I was to learn a valuable business lesson in this transaction. The deal was agreed upon on a Friday, and I was to take possession the following Monday morning. Among the items included in the transaction was grocery stock worth approximately $5,000. When I showed up to begin my new business early Monday morning, one of the neighbors came over and asked me what I was doing.

"I'm opening for business, friend!" I told him.

He scratched his head. "Funny. Thought maybe the place was going outta business, what with all that stuff being hauled away yesterday."

I went in and found that about a fifth of the stock had been removed, and I immediately phoned the real estate agent who had handled the sale and told him it was off unless the price was dropped $1,000 to compensate for what had been taken.

"Let's try to work it out, Mr. Maddox," he said. "I'm sure there's simply a misunderstanding."

A meeting was arranged that afternoon at the office of the lawyer representing the seller. The first thing I did was call the wholesaler who supplied the store. Many items were still under wartime rationing, and I was told the owners were in arrears on ration coupons, which meant I would have to re-establish quotas.

They had lied to me about the ration stamps for meat, sugar, etc. And I was able to prove it to them in the presence of the real estate agent and their attorney. What really aroused my ire was when I complained of their stealing and their totally false statements. Their own lawyer stated that if he had sold such a business that he, too, would remove such merchandise as desired prior to the new owner's taking over. This really shocked me and I jumped from my seat and stormed at the attorney, "If you are that kind of man, then you are just as crooked as these men who have stolen from me." I also added, "You're nothing but a bunch of crooks and having had no experience in dealing with crooks I'm going to try and get someone just as crooked as you are." With that I shoved my chair against the attorney's desk and gave the door a mighty slam on my way out.

I was amazed at the hypocrisy, dishonesty, and cheating and I went back, locked the grocery store and returned to operate the grill until that sale was closed. The real estate agent came to me the following day and told me they had agreed to come down $500.

"I told all of you yesterday that $1,000 worth of stock was stolen out of the store. When that's paid for, we'll close!"

Half an hour later he was back. "All right, Mr. Maddox. They've agreed."

The grocery business was tough. I could not compete with the big chain stores on price, and I did have considerable difficulty in re-establishing the quotas for rationed items. I made up my mind almost immediately that this was not the business for me, and I resold it a month and a half later, at a profit.

My next venture was almost a disaster. A large ice cream distributor had seven Igloo Ice Cream Stores for sale for something like $10,000. Ice cream had been a very profitable item at Lester's Grill, and it seemed to me that *seven* ice cream parlors would be nothing less than a gold mine. My optimism ran away with me. I negotiated a loan, signed the papers, and took over. I soon found that I could not be present at seven separate locations. Employees failed to show up for work, or, when they did, they did not consider honesty the best policy. I sold the stores back to the distributor at a loss and got out of that business.

At this point I paused only long enough to see that I was making a pretty fair living, even with the latest loss, and I was making it not on the operation of the businesses, but in the sale of them. I was in the real estate business and didn't know it.

I then went into real estate as a full-time job, getting my license and working through Atlanta Realty Company. Almost at once I was making money, principally in the sale of residential property. From time to time I bought a piece of property when I thought the price was right and held it until I could turn a profit.

I thought that this was perhaps my place in the world of commerce, and was doing very well indeed. I had bought a 1937 Dodge, which I used in business as well as for the family. One evening in November 1946, with the whole family in the car, I was driving down State Street. The car ahead of me moved to the right and slowed as if to park at the curb. I started by on the left side when, suddenly, the car swerved toward me, apparently having moved to the right only to make a wider arc in the left turn. I cut the wheel sharply to avoid a collision, slamming on the brakes as the cars sideswiped each other. The two girls were in the back seat. Lester, Jr., two years old, was in the front standing between Virginia and me, and the abrupt stop at the moment of collision sent the boy smashing through the windshield onto the hood. The girls were thrown against the seat back but not seriously hurt. Virginia and I, thrown forward by the impact, were stunned momentarily. We got out of the car as quickly as we could, and Virginia pulled the child off the hood. Blood was everywhere, and as I took the boy from her and held his back against me with one hand across his abdomen and the other near his throat, I felt open flesh, and for one horrifying moment I knew that he had been cut completely open.

A young man from a nearby house offered to rush us to nearby Crawford Long Hospital. I asked the first man I saw at the emergency entrance to show me the way.

"Follow me," he said.

As he led us into the emergency room I asked him if he could help me find a doctor immediately, as I did not know if the boy in my arms was dead or alive.

"I'm Dr. Kells Boland, Jr.," he said. "If you haven't already contacted your own doctor I'll be glad to help."

"No, sir," I replied, "I haven't called a doctor. Please do what you can for our son!"

Dr. Boland, assisted by a team of hospital nurses and aides, took the child into the emergency room. The boy was, of course, unconscious. He was in shock and had lost a great deal of blood. Blood was drawn from me, as Lester, Jr., and I had the same type. More than an hour after we arrived, Dr. Boland came out of the operating room and took me aside.

"Mr. Maddox, the child is in deep shock and apparently suffering a serious concussion. He has a number of bad cuts on his head, around his eyes and nose, and his lower lip has almost been severed. I can't promise that he will pull through, but we do have to sew up his cuts."

"I want you to do whatever you feel has to be done," I said. "We'll pray for you and the boy."

Virginia and I remained at the hospital through the long night, praying as hard as we had ever prayed for anything. Dr. Boland had told us if the child made it through the night, his chances of recovery would be good. With the first light of dawn he was still alive, thanks to God, through the skillful hands of Dr. Boland and the hospital staff.

I squeezed Virginia's hand as we gazed down at the small form lying in the hospital bed. "Hi, son. This is Daddy. You're going to be all right! Yes, sir, you're going to be just fine!" I smiled, finding it hard to hold back the tears of thankfulness. His face was covered with gauze dressings with only one eye visible to us. That eye looked up at us, and I knew that Lester was trying to smile back.

Virginia was five months pregnant at the time of the accident, and her already frail health was not helped by this. There was serious concern on the part of her doctor that she might lose the baby. This, and young Lester's severe injuries, caused her to become almost despondent. She was unable to manage the house and look after the children in her condition, and I was required at home more than ever. In sales, time away from work meant money lost and now the savings we had managed to accumulate began to dwindle away, and I had to sell off the small pieces of land I had been able to buy.

One piece, located on Hemphill Avenue, proved to be especially difficult to move, which was understandable when its drawbacks were considered. For one thing, the neighborhood had very little to offer. The property itself lay ten or twelve feet below street level, and while it had been a convenient dumping ground for years, the trash and junk deposited there seemed to disappear in the hole rather than to fill it.

I decided I would have to improve it, and I would do well to improve it in such a way that it would provide me with a means of livelihood should it still fail to sell. I drew up plans for a building, but before I could proceed I had to negotiate a loan, and I began making the rounds of banks and savings and loan associations. My record in this effort was perfect: I was turned down by one and all, including the Small Business Administration. I began to try the loan departments of insurance companies, and after being rejected by a number of these, I found myself one morning in the office of Elbert Reeves of Jefferson Standard Life. I explained my plans to him and said that I needed $12,500 in order to fill the land and put up my building. He had me fill out a formal application.

"I'll get this right off to the home office, Mr. Maddox, and I'll be in touch as soon as I get a reply."

Several days later, to my amazement, he called and said I was approved for a permanent loan on the property.

My plan was to put up a building and equip it as a restaurant, and if I was not able to sell it by the time it was finished, I would get it started and sell it as a going business as I had Lester's Grill.

We had to have a name, something a little more imaginative than Lester's Grill. One night I was mulling over a few ideas, putting together various words and phrases.

One caught my fancy, and I asked Virginia, "Listen to this, honey. 'Picknick at Pickwick.' How's that sound?"

She thought about it. "What does 'Pickwick' mean?"

"Well, nothing, actually. But it rhymes and it sounds good."

"The Pickwick Restaurant," she said, getting the sound of it. "It is sort of catchy, isn't it?"

Chapter 3

Pickrick Says

It never did become the Pickwick. That name was already registered in Atlanta and I wanted something entirely unique and my own, and I continued to mull over possible names while going ahead with construction. I was my own prime contractor, architect, engineer, and I did a lot of the sawing, nailing, and bricklaying as well. Even so, it was not long before I found I had what the government calls a "cost over-run," and I went to Jefferson Standard and managed to get my loan commitment increased to $17,500. By the time construction was finished, everything I had was invested in the place, and I had no prospective buyer in sight. I had a completed restaurant facility, and I was obviously back in business, at least, for the time being.

All I needed now was the name. I could not get "Pickwick" entirely out of my mind, and leafing through the dictionary one night I happened onto a word that fell right into place. I kept "Pick," which my dictionary defined as "to select, to eat fastidiously," and now to go with that I had discovered "Rick," which meant "to pile up or to heap, to amass."

Pickrick! It sounded exactly right, and not only that, it provided a slogan as well, "You pick it out, we'll rick it up." Picknick at the Pickrick!

I put in stock, hired cooks, waiters, busboys, dishwashers, and on December 7, 1947, the Pickrick opened its doors for business.

From the day I began filling the vacant lot preparatory to building I had been getting advice from numerous friends and acquaintances as to the poor judgment in putting a restaurant there. This seemed to be backed by the complete lack of interest to any would-be buyer. One astute businessman later told me that when he drove down Hemphill Avenue on his way to work each day he watched the progress of the restaurant operation with an eye toward picking the building up as soon as the restaurant folded for use as a display for his wholesale equipment business.

He had good reason for this feeling, and it probably came closer to happening than he ever knew. The first year of operation, working seven days a week, Virginia—when her health permitted—and I put in nearly 11,000 hours with a resulting net income of $1,719. Figured on an hour rate, this was little improvement over the three cents I had made as a boy bagging peanuts for the circus.

If there was a single factor, other than hard work, that kept the Pickrick alive in its infancy, it was that Hemphill Avenue comprised a section of U. S. Highway 41 going north and south through the city. Residents of the immediate vicinity, men from the steel mill, the stockyards, rail yards, and students from nearby Georgia Tech, were unable to eat out regularly, even at the low prices we charged, and the bulk of our business at that time depended on the through traffic.

The restaurant grew slowly but steadily, and all the while it remained for sale with the price escalating upward with the increase in business. Just as it appeared to be over the hump and on its way, something happened that came very close to closing it down, along with numerous other small businesses along Hemphill and adjacent streets. U.S. 41 was rerouted off to Hemphill and on to Spring Street, a mile or so to the east. I was completely dumbfounded by this action by the Georgia Highway Department, as were the other merchants who saw the traffic flow suddenly dwindle to a trickle.

We had to make our voices heard, or die; it was that simple. Somehow the leadership of the merchants' group fell to me and I contacted the highway department, only to become enmeshed in the bureaucratic red tape. I was soon spending almost all my time attempting to reverse what had been done, and managed to get the southbound traffic routed back onto Hemphill Avenue. The problem was by no means solved, however, as many of the businesses dependent on the through traffic had been marginal even when the flow was two-way. I could see no sense whatever in putting the additional load on Spring Street, which carried a great deal of local traffic anyhow. There were nine traffic lights where there had been only two, and the route was longer.

I decided to go right to the top, to Jim Gillis himself, the long-time, powerful highway commissioner. A friend, County Commissioner Archie Lindsey, helped set up an appointment, but the meeting accomplished nothing.

"You might as well stop bothering me," Gillis told me flatly. "The decision has been made to keep 41 the way it is, and that's all there is to it!"

All my arguments seemed to do nothing more than increase the inflexibility of Gillis and the department, and that night I took what appeared to be the only remaining channel. I wrote a long letter to Georgia's junior senator, Herman Talmadge, detailing the whole episode. I have never spoken to Senator Talmadge about this in the years since, but the letter seemed to have produced what nothing else had done. A few days later I received a telegram from the state highway department informing me that U.S. 41 was to be rerouted onto Hemphill, both north and south, as soon as the signs could be changed.

Business soon got back to normal, but it had been a real pinch and if it had continued much longer it would have closed the Pickrick and a lot of other businesses. It was a vivid example of what can be accomplished by the perseverance of ordinary citizens over great odds.

On a cold, blustery day in March 1948, Lester, Jr., at the age of four, was almost lost to us. Virginia and I were at the Pickrick, and the child was at home with our maid, Dolores. He found some matches and was striking them outside the house in the wind. Suddenly, his clothes caught fire. He beat at the flames in terror, and, unable to put them out in that fashion, ran to the front yard, where he had the presence of mind to turn on the hydrant. By that time the gusty winds had fanned the flames to such an extent that they were engulfing his upper body and head. He was unable to get under the stream of water and fled in pain and panic to the back-yard, where he gave up his fight. It was then that Dolores heard the child screaming and found him standing, his arms stretched helplessly above his head, his body wreathed in flames, and she rushed out with a blanket, covered him quickly, and put out the fire. Her quick action undoubtedly saved the boy's life.

Virginia's health had shown steady improvement, however, and with the return of Highway 41 the Pickrick also was gaining steadily. It was no overnight success; as late as 1950 customers' cars were still getting stuck in the parking lot during rainy weather because I was unable to complete the paving.

With the steady increase in business I gradually added onto the original building. In 1949 I began running advertisements in the Saturday editions of the Atlanta Newspapers. The Saturday editions were shunned by retail merchants because of the relatively small circulation, and the fact that they had little advertising other than the Sunday church ads was one of the reasons I chose them. I figured that even if fewer people read it, my ad would have a high incidence of readership because of the lack of other ads competing for the readers' attention. Also, the rates were lower. I had my own ideas about what the ad should be to attract attention, a mix of commentary, political observations, opinions, and, of course, the Pickrick's menu and prices.

The Cox Atlanta newspaper monopoly, the *Constitution* and the *Journal,* were adamantly opposed to my conservative and segregationist philosophy, and I found myself continually running into obstacles from the people I had to buy my advertising space from. My ads were so controversial that the papers had their general counsel check every word before they would run them. At one time they became so infuriated at what I had written, the advertising director called me and told me they would not run any more Pickrick ads.

"Why?" I asked him. "What's your reason for this?"

"We don't have to give a reason," he replied.

Being a strong supporter of private enterprise, I realized it was their right and their prerogative to reject or accept what customers they wished.

But I also had a choice, and I chose to run the rejected ads in small, independent weekly papers in the metro area, and I ran the ads with an additional heading which read: *"The Atlanta Newspapers Refused to Run This Ad!"*

Evidently, the *Journal* and *Constitution* re-evaluated their decision, for three weeks later their ad department called and requested that I resume submitting ads to them. Their earlier rejection of Pickrick ads must have been costly to them in more ways than one, for I resubmitted three ads they had previously refused, and they ran them.

They were in a dilemma, however, because my ads began to jack up the circulation of the weak Saturday editions; in fact, according to the Atlanta Newspapers themselves, my Pickrick ad was the most widely read "column" in either edition. The advertising departments of the papers received many requests to "lay out ads like Pickrick," and the advertising director told me that my ads were a topic of discussion at various local and regional trade meetings.

My objective was not to bring advertisers to the newspapers, but customers to the restaurant, and "Pickrick Says" did this. Our supper business had been slow, and it began to pick up. It was always my policy to meet my customers and chat with them and now the conversation got around to my ads many times. Most folks told me they liked the ads and agreed with much in the views I expressed. Others felt not quite so agreeable. One gentleman who had been a regular lunch customer for quite some time buttonholed me in the presence of a large number of my customers and in a loud and angry voice said:

"Maddox, if you don't stop running those blankety-blank ads, you're gonna lose me as a customer!"

"Well, I'm not gonna stop the ads, and I really don't think you'll stop eating at the Pickrick. You know as well as I do that five of your employees quit me a while back, and I heard two of them have now got ulcers and the other three, heart trouble. They miss this good Pickrick cooking! I don't believe you want to take a chance of longing for this good food like they're doing now!"

It was my practice to move about among the tables, refilling coffee cups and stopping for a word here and there. A fellow motioned to me one evening and when I paused at his table he told me very bluntly that he just plain did not like me.

"Why?" I asked him.

"Why!" he snorted. "Because you're *against* everything!"

"No, sir," I replied. "If I'm against certain things, that's because of the things I'm for. I'll tell you some of the things I'm not against; I'm not against God, freedom, the United States, rights of private property and free enterprise, and free speech. And I'm not against you. I let you go through the line and sit down here to eat and you ought to be glad I'm not throwing you out. About the only thing I'm really against is Communism." I looked him straight in the eye. "How do you stand on Communism?"

His face began to turn purple, and he stood up, threw his napkin on the table, and stalked out.

From the beginning my aim had been to make the Pickrick more than just another family restaurant. I bought the best meats, poultry, and vegetables, and kept the prices down, depending on volume for the success of the Pickrick. I was the first in Atlanta to offer free refills on coffee and tea. I had a public-address system and offered many sorts of prizes. One month I offered fifty dollars to the family who brought the youngest baby to eat at the Pickrick, and a young couple with their three-day-old daughter stopped by on their way home from the maternity ward to have dinner and collect. There was a setting bantam hen on a nest at the front door and a prize for the person who guessed closest to when and how many of the eggs hatched. From time to time I would pick up the microphone and ask some couple entering the cafeteria line, "What kind of chicken do you like best?" And if they answered, "Pickrick skillet-fried chicken!" they would eat free. One year I gave away more than 8,000 free dinners this way.

I have always been a firm believer in truth in advertising. Often on the menu we would have chicken gizzards, which, while not the most popular portion of the bird, were nourishing and inexpensive. I began to notice many people saying that the gizzards were tough, so I added, in parentheses, (tough) after *gizzards* on the menu. One evening I stopped to pour fresh coffee for a nice little lady and she smiled up at me.

"There are a lot of things I like about the Pickrick," she said. "But what I like the most is that you're honest and truthful."

"Thank you, ma'am, but what do you mean?"

She picked up a chicken gizzard from her plate with her fork. "Your menu says these are tough, and you're right. They're the toughest things I ever ate in my life!"

The way I operated the place, mingling and talking with the customers, I thought most of them knew me. One evening shortly after eleven o'clock, which was our closing time, I had on a little white Pickrick hat and was tidying up a bit with a broom as I let a couple out and locked the door after them. A fellow at a nearby table motioned to me.

"How come you're locking up?" he said.

"We always close our dining room at eleven," I told him.

"Since when?"

"Since we opened for business."

He shook his head and took a bite of chicken. "You don't know what you're talking about. This place used to be open twenty-four hours a day. How long you been working here?"

I shifted the broom from one hand to the other and adjusted my cap. "You might say I was one of the first employees. I helped plan the building and open the restaurant."

"Well, you don't know what you're talking about! Back when old Lester Maddox ran it, it stayed open twenty-four hours!"

"Oh? You know Lester Maddox?"

"*Know* him? Been knowing him all my life! We were friends in school!"

I moved away, sweeping, thinking maybe I should mix with my customers a little more. He went on eating, unaware that the fellow he had been talking to was the same old friend he had known all his life.

My "Pickrick Says" ads were doing as good a job for the newspapers as they were for me. The size of the Saturday edition had grown from a dozen or so pages to two or three times that, which gave advertising officials at the Atlanta Newspapers the brilliant idea of an Amusement and Entertainment Section, in which the ads of eating establishments would be featured. I was told that my ads would be run in the section. This obviously would be detrimental to the Pickrick and I rejected the idea of being on a page with all the others who, incidentally, were there because of Pickrick in the first place.

Later, I was told that they were going to begin charging me on the national rate rather than the lower local rate that other retail merchants enjoyed because I had so much to say about the national political scene in my ads. Rather than become angry and quit, I told them to double or triple my rate if they wished, but to send me a letter explaining why they were charging me more than other merchants. Just before the deadline I was advised that "the board" had held a special meeting and decided that the old rate would prevail. Even though I had won another skirmish with them, they no longer allowed me to pick the location of my ad in the paper. This meant that my ad might appear on the sports page, or with the comics or obituaries.

I don't think the newspapers ever really knew whether they wanted my ads or not. On the earlier occasion when they had turned some of them down and I had run them in suburban weeklies, the Atlanta papers had relented and run the ads, and publisher Ralph McGill stated to the effect that the paper had searched its soul and had found there would be less trouble in running the ads than in not doing so, and, besides, it was not important.

My response was that the search had not been of their souls, but of their wallets, which were not found to be as thick as before.

The ultra-liberal Atlanta *Constitution,* with McGill as publisher and his protégé Eugene Patterson as editor, never let up attacking Lester Maddox. To them I was a bigot, racist, and just about anything else they could think of to make me out as some kind of devil. I decided to find out something, and one day I went down to the newspaper's office on Forsyth Street. Starting at the front door I made my way through the place looking for black faces. If I was a racist while employing more than forty-five blacks among my sixty-five employees, many in supervisory jobs, surely this liberal paper must be staffed predominantly by Negroes. Yet everywhere I looked there were white faces, with only an occasional black pushing a broom. There were no black secretaries, office workers, or reporters.

Later, when I brought this to the attention of the public, an employee invited me to visit the editorial offices of the newspaper. When I arrived there, I found that one of the white secretaries had had her face blacked Amos-and-Andy style. "Now you can't claim we don't have a black in a prominent position at this newspaper," I was told.

I have many friends and supporters working for the Atlanta Newspapers, probably as high a percentage as in any large company in Georgia. This hypocritical action from an executive, however, was not an isolated incident. I have found it to be this way in so many positions of leadership, in business, government, education, and even in the church, where so many of these leaders preach one thing and practice the opposite.

My goal since childhood had been to become a successful businessman. Thanks to the wonderful country I lived in and its Constitution, which afforded every citizen the opportunity of reaching this goal to whatever limits his efforts and God-given abilities would carry him, I had become what I set out to be. The Pickrick was a success. By 1957 we were serving some half a million people annually.

As every schoolchild knows, however, this land of opportunity did not just happen. Brave men and women fought and died to create it and many more down through the years fought and died to preserve it. I believe that any man who simply accepts this as something that is his due and who does not actively work in some way to protect it, suffers from shortsightedness and selfishness. I had then, as now, a deep and abiding interest in protecting the conservatism and individualism that were responsible for my own success.

Up until this time I had never seriously considered running for any elective office. I had been greatly disturbed, as had many other citizens, by reports of corruption in Altanta's government. Prior to the Democratic primary in 1957 Atlanta was scandalized by reported lottery payoffs to a number of Atlanta policemen, and it appeared that the time was ripe for a clean sweep of the long entrenched city hall crowd, headed by Mayor William B. Hartsfield, and the election of a new mayor.

Fulton County Commission Chairman Archie Lindsey was that man. I had known him for many years, as a Sunday School teacher at North Atlanta Baptist Church, as a friend, and as a customer at the Pickrick. I worked hard in behalf of Lindsey's candidacy, including the hosting of a fund-raising dinner at the Pickrick. Law and order was the burning issue, and with the blight of the police scandal fresh in the voters' minds it seemed that Lindsey would run away with the election on the platform of reform alone.

It did not work out this way, however. Perhaps the power of the establishment that backed Hartsfield was underestimated; perhaps Lindsey ran too mild a race against an incumbent. In fact, I was disappointed and disgusted that the alarming growth of crime and lawlessness in the city was not even made an issue in the primary. I feel until this day that this was the *major* issue at that time, and if it had been brought out into the open Archie Lindsey would have become Atlanta's mayor. Whatever the cause, Hartsfield edged him out by taking aproximately 53 per cent of a total vote of some 70,000, and emerged as the Democratic nominee.

In 1957 the Republican Party was virtually non-existent in Atlanta. The primary was, to all intents and purposes, the election. The general election to be held in November was, in this case, little more than a legal formality.

However, this legal formality allowed for entry by petition. The signatures of 2 per cent of the registered voters on a petition would place a candidate's name on the general election ballot. For the first time in my life I began to give serious consideration to running for elective office. I was forty-two years old, had no political experience other than my years of active support of other candidates, and even my public speaking experience was limited to lodge meetings and the like. If I chose to make the attempt, I would be facing one of the ablest politicians and orators, not only in the city of Atlanta, but in the Southeast.

If you're going to fight an orator, you've got to fight him on his own grounds. I called the Dale Carnegie Courses and enrolled in the next class that started. I suppose I had a certain amount in innate ability, and I did well. I announced my candidacy before the course was half over.

Chapter 4

The First Three

Like most citizens, I had never given serious consideration to being a candidate for any elective office. My political activity consisted of letting my own views be known and in backing the candidates who came closest to sharing my feelings. The Democratic primary of 1957 had seemed to be a perfect opportunity to clean the political machine out of city hall. I—and a great many others—felt that the crime issue would tip the scales in Archie Lindsey's favor, as the police scandal, with all its implications of far-reaching corruption, was a powerful odor in the Alanta air. Lindsey's loss was more than a simple failure; it was a shock.

The issue still remained unresolved, and it still presented an opportunity. I felt that someone had to continue the fight, even though the primary was past. I was convinced that Lindsey had failed to use the tremendous leverage that had been at his disposal, and in fighting as cunning a master of politics as William Hartsfield, failure to use every legitimate advantage was tantamount to giving that advantage over to him. Someone had to make the attempt, and I asked myself: why not Lester Maddox? Shortly after the primary I wrote in my "Pickrick Says" ad:

> AND speaking of the mayor's race I've done about all the building there is room for out here, and being one who likes to build and grow, I've been thinking maybe I could build some highways, some parking areas, finance an airport or two, and do a lot of progressive things—if I could find a job that affords such an opportunity. There is only one job in Atlanta that offers me what I'm interested

and I would like very much to have your comments on
what you think about this idea.

I found that my readers were far from being reticent, and I
received a great deal of encouragement to make the race and this
provided considerable weight to what I did.

I have been a fortunate man in many ways, but the most fortunate thing that ever befell me was Virginia Cox accepting my proposal of marriage. She has been wife, mother, partner, friend, the
most loyal mate a man could want. When I made my decision to
run, Virginia uncomplainingly undertook the burden of man-
aging the Pickrick, aided of course by our children and our loyal
staff of employees, while I set about the task of securing signatures on my petition for a place on the general election ballot.

Being a Democrat, I was violating the unwritten law that the
primary alone was the accepted way of doing this. This not only
assured me of no backing by the party, but of its firm and active
opposition. Without party sanction my campaign would be the sole
responsibility of Lester Maddox and his supporters, which was actually the way I preferred it, as it did not leave me in the debt of
any politicians. People support was all I wanted.

My principal base of operations was the Pickrick, although I did
set up a small petition headquarters in the West End area. At the
outset the Hartsfield forces looked on me as little more than a
nuisance. Mayor Hartsfield was quoted as scoffing at the suggestion that I would get as many as 2,500 votes. This cocksure attitude took a quick change, however, when an Atlanta public relations firm conducting a poll for Mayor Hartsfield showed I was
already in the lead in six of Atlanta's eight wards, and when I announced that I had some 9,000 signatures on my petition, the
lackadaisical attitude of the opposition came to an abrupt halt.
Hartsfield opened a campaign headquarters, an unusual action for
such a long-entrenched official to take. In fact the poll caused such
shock in the political establishment that a meeting was held the
same night of the various facets of power of the city and $25,000
was raised on the spot and pledges of another $25,000 to be raised
within forty-eight hours, which I am confident they did.

I had several times the required number of signatures on my petition, which I kept in the safe at the Pickrick until it was time to
present them officially to the mayor, as required by law. Having

observed the political machine operate in Atlanta for so many years, and having seen the moral decay so clearly manifested by the recent police scandals, I decided to take no chances with the petition, and on the day prior to my presenting the petitions to city hall I hired Brink's to pick them up in an armored truck and keep them overnight for fear someone might attempt to destroy them.

The following day a large number of friends and supporters accompanied me and my family to city hall. The Brinks truck arrived on schedule and the petitions were taken inside and up to the mayor's office by the armed guards.

Hartsfield was summoned from his inner office and he approached me with a look of deep skepticism.

"Mr. Mayor," I said, "I am here to present petition signatures as required by law to enter my name as a candidate for the office of mayor in the general election. I would appreciate a receipt for these signatures, sir."

Hartsfield was not a large man physically, but he loomed large when he chose to do so. He glowered at me. "Mr. Maddox, since I do not know if these are genuine signatures, I cannot give you a receipt for a petition, but only for an *alleged* petition!"

However, I did get my receipt and the mayor had his little joke and I had my first political encounter with the man I would be fighting in the weeks to come. I was to learn quite a lot in the art of politicking at the hands of Bill Hartsfield.

The petitions were duly validated and my candidacy became official. I opened a campaign headquarters of modest dimensions in downtown Atlanta on Peachtree Street. A few doors down the same block, the newly opened Hartsfield headquarters made no pretensions of modesty. Where his was staffed with paid employees and others who had a stake in maintaining the status quo, the Maddox headquarters was manned by myself, my family, friends, and volunteers from the blue-collar and white-collar ranks. The Atlanta "establishment" that stood foursquare behind the continuation of the status quo, personified at the time by Hartsfield, has never run a campaign that suffered from lack of money. Whatever is deemed necessary to do the job, that and more is ready and available. This fact of political life, however, was not so much on the public's mind in 1957 as it has been since Watergate.

My campaign funds were so limited that virtually every expenditure called for a major decision as to whether the money might be better spent elsewhere. The average man, the ordinary citizen, whatever he may be labeled, has never been in a position to donate money for the financing of political campaigns. At least, not in the amounts that are spent when there is no hesitation in spending a million or more dollars to put a man in a $20,000- or $30,000-a-year office for four years. I do not recall a single contribution to my 1957 mayoral campaign in excess of $100, and those that even closely approached that figure could be counted on the fingers of one hand.

The campaign had its official launching at a dinner at the Biltmore Hotel, where I promised several hundred guests that I would throw the corrupt political machine out of city hall when I became mayor. I quickly discovered it was one thing to address my own supporters and campaign workers and quite another even to get an invitation to speak elsewhere. If the two candidates were invited to address a civic club or some other group, all Hartsfield had to do was excuse himself and neither of us would be heard. At the few gatherings where we did meet I attempted to press the issue of Atlanta's growing crime problem and of the apparent lack of effort on the part of the mayor and his administration to put the brakes on.

I was convinced then, and still am, that organized crime could not exist without the condonement, involvement, or knowledge of the mayor.

At one appearance before a Buckhead group I named places that seemed to have immunity from police interference, places where the lottery, bootlegging, prostitution, and other illegal activities were carried on without hindrance by the law. But the mayor sidestepped these issues whenever I brought them up, and threw up an oratorical smoke screen with all the adeptness for which he was so widely renowned. However, I challenged him when he refused to respond and told the group, "He knows if he does he will get the chief of police in trouble, and if the chief talks about it, he will get the mayor in trouble!"

Although a reporter for the Atlanta newspapers, Jack Nelson, had originally exposed the alleged police connections with the illegal lottery, I was unable to get the media to support my conten-

6. In front of the Pickrick after the closing.

7. My one-man march on the Federal Building in Atlanta in March 1965. I carried this sign and several others in relays. (Photo courtesy Wide World Photos)

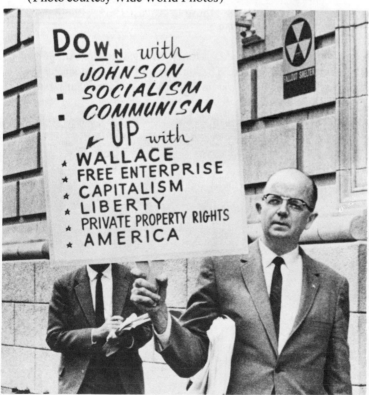

8. Picketing the White House in August 1965. (Photo courtesy Wide World Photos)

9. This was taken at the Henry Grady Hotel in Atlanta on September 28, 1966. The outcome of the Democratic primary for governor was in doubt at this time. That's Larry, Virginia, and Lester, Jr., with me.

10. After I was sworn in as governor in 1967, the whole family gathered for a photograph under the state seal. Virginia's standing next to me, and behind us, left to right, are daughter-in-law Jean; sons Lester, Jr., and Larry; daughter Linda Densmore, and son-in-law Don Densmore. (Photo courtesy Wide World Photos)

11. Georgia Supreme Court Justice Carlton Mobley administering the oath of office at public inauguration ceremonies, January 11, 1967. (Photo courtesy Wide World Photos)

12. The National Governors Conference in St. Thomas, Virgin Islands, October 1967, gave us all a chance to relax, especially in the way we dressed. (Photo courtesy Virgin Islands Government Office of Public Relations)

13. Getting my feet wet at the Virgin Islands Governors Conference.

tions, and with a total campaign fund of less than $10,000 to work with, there was no possibility of publicizing the real issues. With this blackout by the media and the lack of opportunity to debate my opponent I had to go person-to-person with my campaign.

It was not enough, however, for when the vote was tallied after the December 4 election, I had been beaten by Hartsfield and the Atlanta power structure that backed him.

My emotions were mixed, and I wrote in my Pickrick ad several days later:

> PICKRICK SAYS a very close friend of mine, Lester Maddox, got a crazy idea that if a citizen found things in local government looking as though the taxpayer was being mistreated and there were failures and mismanagement on the part of public officials, then the thing to do was to jump in and try to clean things up. WELL, LESTER is a little ignorant. He says he believes in rule by the majority and the people have spoken . . . he will continue as a private citizen, offering himself and his efforts to Atlanta and its citizens whenever called upon.

I had made my run and lost, and I went back to operating the Pickrick, with no thought one way or the other about ever running for office again.

This four-year term of Hartsfield's, not unexpectedly to me, saw the conditions of crime and corruption in Atlanta remain about as they had been. As the end of the term grew near, Hartsfield had not made it known whether he would be a candidate again or not. On the assumption that either Hartsfield or a handpicked successor put forth by the Atlanta power structure would run, I decided to back the man I thought would represent strong conservative opposition, but I soon learned I had misjudged this man, and once more I leaped into the fray, this time in the primary.

At this point there were five announced candidates—Lester Maddox, State Representative M. M. "Muggsy" Smith, State Senator Charlie Brown, Fulton County Commissioner Jim Aldredge, and Howell Smith—and at least one unannounced candidate, which might be Hartsfield again, or the man being mentioned more and more as his chosen successor, Ivan Allen, Jr. I had suspected that he might be the man, for I had heard during the 1957 race that the "establishment" had told Hartsfield they would support him for only one more term, and Hartsfield had agreed he would not run again.

The pressure behind Allen began to build. The Atlanta *Constitution* began to sing his praises, and Atlanta banker Mills Lane, at his own personal expense, polled some 90,000 customers of the Citizens and Southern Bank and announced a very positive Allen movement in the response.

Hartsfield still had not made his intentions publicly known. Ivan Allen later wrote that he went to the mayor with a proposition; Allen would personally put up $10,000 for Hartsfield's campaign, take a leave of absence from his business, and act as campaign manager, or if Hartsfield was not going to run, let it be known so that Allen could begin his own campaign.

The meaning was clear enough. There could only be one "establishment" candidate—Hartsfield or Allen. The seventy-two-year-old mayor, not unexpectedly, chose the second option, and Allen was enthroned as the fair-haired choice of the power structure, acknowledged so by the presidents of Atlanta's five major banks, with a handy and available claque of several hundred employees of his family's office supply business, the Ivan Allen Company, and by his own admission more than enough money to run a "professional" campaign.

Allen later wrote: "I was quite aware that my most serious opposition would come from Lester Maddox . . . a 10th grade dropout who ran a blue-collar fried-chicken restaurant called the Pickrick [and who] had sprung out of the lower- and middle-class white neighborhood suddenly when the Supreme Court handed down its decision on school desegregation. As polarization set in, his star rose higher. Undoubtedly he would scream 'nigger-nigger-nigger' throughout the campaign."

This last accusation, of course, was absurd, and nothing more than a diversionary tactic. The campaign itself proved otherwise, that my platform was for cleaning up government and eradicating crime. I *was* a tenth-grade dropout, having done so, as I pointed out earlier, because of the necessity of helping to provide for my brothers and sisters after my father lost his job in the steel mill. Mr. Allen's own high school education came very close to early termination but for the good fortune of having been born with a silver spoon in his mouth. To quote him: "My record at Boys' High the first two years was so bad that I doubt if they would have let me stay in school if my father hadn't been such a prominent citizen."

It would seem, then, that his snide allusion to Lester Maddox as a "dropout" running a "blue-collar fried-chicken restaurant" was simply his own form of bigotry.

The race was, however, between Allen and Maddox. Early in the campaign he attempted to brand me. At a rally at the McLendon Elementary School he turned from the podium and aimed a finger at me.

"Mr. Maddox, you hear this! You represent a group that would bring another Little Rock to Atlanta!" The tirade went on, following the lines already well established by the Atlanta Newspapers and other opponents of mine. When he was done attacking me, I pointed out to the crowd that Allen was once more attempting to throw up a smoke screen by attempting to create a racial issue, and that his reason for this was the fact that he represented the group that benefited from corrupt government, the cleaning up of which was one of my central platform planks.

From time to time I characterized Allen as the Peachtree Peacock and the candidate ordained by Atlanta's czars of finance as the next mayor of the city. "And I have something for you, sir," I said at one rally, motioning for him to stand. I pulled a pair of Virginia's hose from my pocket. "Here's a pair of silk stockings for the Silk Stocking candidate!" I said, handing them to him.

He took them, as there was little else he could do, but as the crowd laughed he said under his breath, "You keep up this sort of thing, Maddox, and I'll get even with you!"

He attempted to make good his promise shortly afterward at a Jaycee-sponsored rally at Campbellton Plaza in southwest Atlanta. Turning to me at the end of his allotted speaking time, he said, "Mr. Maddox, when this is over are you going to add good hot dogs and hamburgers to the good fried chicken you serve at your restaurant?"

"Mr. Allen," I replied, "I'm glad you recognize we've got good food at the Pickrick, but as good as it is, it's nothing compared to the good government this city will have when I'm mayor. And I'm not surprised to hear you talking about chicken; as many eggs as you've laid around town, it's time you started cackling!"

The real issues of the campaign were obscured in the Atlanta media. The Cox newspaper monopoly of the *Journal* and *Constitution* never let up in characterizing me as a racist and a demagogue. They made no effort to distinguish between a segregationist —which I was then and am today—and a racist—which I was not then and never will be. The fact that in addition to my major pledge to wage war on crime, I was strongly for slum clearance, expressways, revitalization of the city with such things as a stadium, concert hall, sports arena, better salaries for city employees, and many other constructive and forward-looking proposals was totally ignored by them in their determination to create an image of Lester Maddox of their own design. Their approach was basically simple: Ivan Allen would wear the white hat, Lester Maddox the black hat.

As for demagoguery and racism, there was no lack of it in the campaign, but it was slyly practiced by the hypocritical newspapers, some religious leaders, and some of the leaders in business, industry, and government in pushing their handpicked candidate.

On September 13, 1961, Atlanta voters went to the polls and the result was surprising to few. Of some 101,000 votes cast, approximately 39,000 went to Allen, 21,000 to Lester Maddox, with the remainder scattered among the other candidates. With no one receiving a majority, Ivan Allen and I were thrown into a runoff.

The runoff was, if anything, more predictable than the primary itself. The Negro bloc vote, which had been split between Allen and Smith earlier, now went for Allen, 36,000 strong. The final count was some 64,000 for Allen, 36,000 for Maddox. The power structure, aligned with the news media, proved again to be an unbeatable combination. At least, in that election.

I met the mayor-elect that evening as I arrived for an interview at the Atlanta *Constitution* newsroom. When I had conceded the election to Ivan Allen, one of the newsmen asked me what my plans were for the future.

I laughed. "I don't know. Maybe I'll run for governor," I told him.

Governor Ernest Vandiver's term was coming to a close the following year, 1962, and I did give some serious thought to entering the race. I was still absolutely convinced that a man unfettered by political debts of any sort could make a positive contribution to good government. While I had been beaten my first two times out, I did not feel that it was so much the lack of political ties, or the lack of support from the power structure of the city that was to blame as it was the lack of fair treatment by the major media serving the voters of Atlanta. I do not mean *favorable* coverage, but simply honest, objective, balanced reporting. They chose to look upon my conservative stand as a danger to the community rather than an effort to stand up for and protect the rights of the people I intended to represent—meaning *all* Atlantans. I felt, though, that even in losing I had contributed by giving the citizens an opportunity to hear the other side.

Atlanta, with the lip-service liberalism of the power structure and the Cox monopoly, was obviously a rough row to hoe for a conservative Democrat in the 1960s.

However, the state of Georgia was another matter. I made my decision to run in the upcoming 1962 election—but not for governor. Former Governor Marvin Griffin, a conservative, was already pitted against a moderate, Carl Sanders, a young lawyer and legislator from Augusta, and I felt that my entry into that race would cause many Griffin supporters to feel that I had been planted by the Sanders faction in order to split the strong conservative vote.

I tossed my hat in as a candidate for lieutenant governor. The two mayoral races and my widely distributed Pickrick ads assured me that I was not entirely unknown around the state. But I did have a problem: I had been born in Atlanta and had spent almost my entire life in Georgia. But I had never found time for travel even around my own state and I knew few people outside Atlanta. And, of course, there was the ever present problem of campaign funds. I considered printing small placards with my name and picture on them, but after observing the huge billboards of the more affluent candidates I simplified my plan. There would be no pictures in the voting booths, only names, and I had posters printed, at a cost of about two cents each, which read simply:

MADDOX

MADDOX

MADDOX

I filled my Mercury station wagon with these and other pieces of campaign literature, and set out alone with a road map. On occasion one or the other of two good friends, J. L. Allen and S. O. "Buster" Sutton, went along with me when their own time would permit. With virtually no campaign treasury, not only was I unable to pay them but they provided for their own food and lodging.

At every town along our way I would go everywhere people were to be found—barbershops, drugstores, gas stations, beauty shops, factories, homes. At traffic lights I would walk up to the cars and introduce myself. "My name's Lester Maddox! I hear there's a rumor going around that eight other men are running for lieutenant governor! If you hear that, just don't pay any attention! Remember Lester Maddox!"

On the roadside when we came to a large billboard bearing the likeness of one of my opponents, we stopped and tacked up three or four MADDOX placards nearby. I figured if the huge billboard caught the eyes of passersby, they could not miss seeing the little placards in the immediate vicinity, and about fifty cents worth of my two-cent posters would be just as effective as several hundred dollars' worth of billboards.

There was strong opposition in the race. Several contenders were well-known statewide politicians whose names, if not exactly household words, were certainly widely recognized. Peter Zack Geer, the dynamic young executive secretary to the incumbent governor, began as the favorite. Despite his youth, Geer was a veteran politician with important contacts throughout the state's Democratic Party. He was a segregationist, a lawyer by trade, and a spellbinding orator. Just as Ivan Allen and I had quickly pulled ahead of the pack the previous year, Peter Zack and I became the men to beat in 1962. This emergence of two segregationists immediately brought down the wrath of the Atlanta Newspapers, who continued to preach one thing and practice another.

At a major Atlanta rally, one of my major opponents attempted to put me down in somewhat the same way Ivan Allen had sneered at my being a "10th grade dropout." He pounded home the point that his legal training and background were of incalculable value to the man gaining the office of lieutenant governor, leaving the audience to weigh my shortcomings for itself.

When it came my turn to speak, I addressed myself directly to my opponent. "What you say, sir, is true. Being a legal scholar can be a fine asset, but such training is not always used in the proper direction. In fact, some of the best legal minds in the country are out there at the end of Boulevard in the Federal Penitentiary, and I do not doubt at all that there are countless others not quite so brilliant on the outside who should be there."

Campaigning for a statewide office in Georgia is no job for a man who prefers short hours. With no political machinery to back me up—a lack which I preferred—and precious little money, time was the only substitute available to me, and I utilized almost every hour of every day. I had no paid campaign workers, no advance men down the line preparing for my arrival. I wrote my own speeches, tacked up my own posters, and gratefully accepted whatever help and support my friends and backers were able to provide, well aware that they were doing all they could.

There were times when this multiplicity of jobs created odd situations. One night about one o'clock, J. L. Allen and I pulled the station wagon into a motel in south Georgia. While J.L. slept in preparation of the long drive next day, I worked another two hours writing a speech, went to bed, and we were up at seven and on our way. As always, we pulled off the highway at every likely spot to tack up posters, and it was not until we had reached the rally in the next town and I was ready to step up to the microphone that I remembered in the wee hours of the morning I had jotted my notes on the back of a MADDOX poster because I was out of notepaper, and my speech was far down the country highway nailed firmly to the trunk of a Georgia pine. Fortunately, I have seldom been at a loss for words, and my speech on that occasion was delivered extemporaneously.

It was a long, hot summer of the sort that seems reserved for election years, and on September 12 more than three quarters of a million Georgians made their way to the polls. The vote was fragmented among the nine candidates for lieutenant governor—as had been expected—and Peter Zack Geer and I, having received more than the others, went into a runoff.

Carl Sanders won the Democratic nomination for governor and he threw his support behind Geer. This was of tremendous value to Geer, as Sanders was a popular choice. I recalled earlier in the summer, at a meeting of the Georgia Municipal Association at Jekyll Island, Sanders took me aside after the speeches were made. "Everywhere I go," he said, "I hear more and more talk of a Sanders-Maddox ticket."

"I'm glad to hear it," I said. "In fact, I've been hearing a lot of that, too. But I also hear a lot about a Griffin-Maddox ticket!"

I did not believe in seeking the support of candidates in other races, or of offering them mine, even though my aligning with Carl Sanders at that time might well have resulted in my becoming lieutenant governor.

There were some strange bedfellows in Georgia before it was over. The man who was perhaps my most virulent critic, Atlanta mayor Ivan Allen, must have found himself in something of a dilemma with no liberals running for the post. Such was his hatred for me, however, he chose to support whoever was running against me and he took a stance of "stop Maddox."

The odds were truly against me now; the traditional courthouse Democrats, men in powerful posts in state agencies, and even the Atlanta Newspapers, finding themselves in the same dilemma as the mayor, swallowed hard and pronounced Mr. Geer to be the lesser of the evils, as they saw it. When the runoff votes were counted after a light turnout, it was Geer 225,000, Maddox 182,000.

I had run my third race, and had lost again. But there was far more to it than simply losing. With all the odds I had made an impressive showing. The political machine was dead set against me, and it had beat me again. However, I did not look upon the three strikes as meaning Lester Maddox was out.

Chapter 5

The Mid-Sixties—Time of Turmoil

Between the noon and evening meals at the Pickrick, Virginia and I would often go home. One Saturday afternoon during this break I was mowing the lawn when I received a very painful insect bite. It became swollen and inflamed and caused considerable discomfort, but I did not feel that it was serious enough to require medical attention, so when my chores were finished I showered, dressed, and we returned to the restaurant to take care of the usual Saturday night business. It was well past midnight when we got home and went to bed. The hours that followed remain a virtual blank in my memory.

Not long after lying down, I got out of bed, stumbled, and sprawled forward onto the hardwood floor, driving a tooth completely through my upper lip. Virginia immediately got out of bed and came to me. I was unconscious and bleeding profusely from the cut lip. She quickly telephoned Dr. George Paulk, a chiropractor and friend who lived nearby. He came as quickly as he could, and as he attempted to stop the flow of blood he told Virginia to call for an ambulance.

I have a faint recollection of being in the ambulance, and then nothing more until the following afternoon. I came to in the unfamiliar surroundings of a hospital room. Virginia stood beside the bed, smiling down at me.

"You had a bad fall, Lester," she said.

I tried to speak and was immediately aware of the injuries to my face and mouth.

"The doctors are running some tests," she went on.

"Tests? What kind of tests?"

My personal physician, Dr. Grant Wilmer, overheard me as he

came into the room. "Routine tests, Mr. Maddox," he said in reply to my question. He asked me a number of things and he seemed particularly interested in the fact that I had no memory of getting out of bed just prior to the fall.

The following two days were spent on tests of all sorts—blood tests, co-ordination tests, questions, something called a "brain scan," and many more. I was becoming impatient to go home when, in midmorning, Dr. Wilmer stopped by. Virginia and the children were with me, and I immediately sensed by the look on Dr. Wilmer's face that he might have some news I had rather not hear.

"We've checked and rechecked certain tests," he began.

"And it's serious?" I interrupted.

"It could be. The tests strongly indicate a possible brain tumor. Of course, we'll want the opinion of additional specialists."

"If the tests prove what you think, then I may not make it?"

"There'll be further testing, but I would be doing you a disservice, Mr. Maddox, if I failed to tell you and your family that if these results are substantiated, things do not look good."

Virginia reached out and took my hand, bravely trying to hold back the tears.

"I understand, Doctor," I said. I tightened my fingers on my wife's hand. "Thank you for being so straightforward with me."

The long series of tests had gradually alerted me to the possibility of a serious condition, but even so, the shock and sense of finality in the doctor's words were sobering. I felt no sense of despair or panic. My unshakable belief in God and in the wisdom of His actions allowed no place for such feelings. The doctor left us alone and I talked to Virginia and the children as they all stood mutely at the bedside, and did my best to cheer them up even under these gloomy tidings.

"We must not be sad. We must be thankful for the blessings of our having been together for the years we have."

The boys, Lester, Jr., and Larry, blinked back their tears. Ginny and Linda were not able to. I prayed to God in my heart as I looked on the faces of my wife and children, thanking Him for my life and the blessings and opportunities He had bestowed upon me. *Lord, if you can use me best in death, here I am, ready. If Your will is to use me best in life, I promise You, dear God, that I will spend the rest of my life trying my best to live for You and in giv-*

ing my testimony for You if I walk away from this bed alive. And I will never cease speaking up for this country, speaking up for what I believe to be right, and against what I believe to be wrong.

I was released from the hospital and Dr. Wilmer contacted a specialist and scheduled further tests shortly afterward at Piedmont Hospital. I went back with the same prayer and commitment I had made earlier, prepared for the worst. The tests were run and evaluated by the doctors, and finally Virginia and I sat in the office to learn the results.

The doctor placed a thick folder on the desk. "The report is excellent, Mr. Maddox. These tests show absolutely no trace of what was so strongly indicated originally. In short, you do not have a brain tumor. I do not fully understand the initial results, but can assure you now that you are a completely healthy man in that respect."

I could hardly believe what I had heard. Later, thinking back, I wondered if the severe insect bite I had received while working in my yard might not have caused some reaction that led to my getting out of bed that night and falling. Perhaps, the doctors explained, the fall itself had resulted in a concussion, which could have been interpreted in the tests as a possible tumor.

Whatever it might have been, as Virginia and I walked out of the hospital, hand in hand, I humbly gave thanks to God for showing me His decision as He had and I renewed the vow I had made. As I had done so many times before, I asked that He give me wisdom, guide me, and use me for His purposes.

When I had originally been taken to St. Joseph's Infirmary after my fall, a plastic surgeon, Dr. William Huger, had been called to sew up the bad cut on my lip. He explained that a blood vessel in the lip had been severed and in all likelihood this portion of the lip would die and a small scar would remain when the healthy flesh grew together where the dead flesh was lost.

"I'll be more than happy if I come out of this whole thing with only a small portion of my lip gone," I said. And I reminded him that on more than one occasion I had been accused of having too much lip anyhow.

The Pickrick was flourishing, and the Lester Maddox family, while far from wealthy, was enjoying the fruits of long years of labor and the opportunities afforded by America. But trouble was on the horizon. Early in 1964 civil rights agitators began their crackdown on the businessmen of Atlanta, and it immediately became apparent that the elected leadership of the city was going to do little or nothing to protect the rights of private property. In January a popular downtown restaurant, Leb's, was literally taken over by gangs of civil rights militants, both black and white, and this incredible action was taken with the full co-operation of the Atlanta Police Department.

Mr. Leb pleaded with the authorities to evict the rabble who had forced their way into his place of business, but his pleas fell on deaf ears. It was not that the police were not on the scene—they were. What they did do was prevent customers from going into the restaurant, thus effectively shutting off Leb's source of income. The demonstrators showed absolutely no respect for private property. They destroyed furniture and fixtures, urinated in food containers, and all this within view of the city's duly constituted enforcers of the law.

I could not believe the sight that met my eyes as I stood on the sidewalk across the street from the restaurant. I was told that the police were allowing no one to cross the street, and were making no effort to remove those on the other side. One of the officers in the street I recognized as a Pickrick customer, and rather than have him tell me I could not cross, I waited until his attention was in another direction, then dashed across and slipped into the restaurant, where I found Mr. Leb in a state of utter shock. He told me what had been happening at his place of business, how he could neither open nor close. The police would not force the demonstrators out, and they would not let his regular customers in.

"This is America, Mr. Maddox!" he said. "How can this be happening!"

Apparently some of the demonstrators had recognized me when I entered Leb's, for they began to chant: *"Maddox is next! Maddox is next! Maddox is next!"*

I assured Mr. Leb that he had whatever support I could provide, and then I went back out to the street. Several so-called "ministers" participating in the destruction of this man's business immediately singled me out. They and hundreds of their fellow pickets jammed the sidewalks all around the building, denying access to anyone.

"We're not just gonna shut you down, Maddox!" they screamed. "We're gonna make you lose everything you got!"

I noticed several white policemen talking to a black officer, and a moment later he moved away from them and approached me. "You have to move on, Mr. Maddox," he said. "Got to clear this area."

"Officer, these people have been here since *yesterday,* and they aren't being cleared out of the area. When you tell *them* to move, that's when I'll move on!"

"That's a police order, Mr. Maddox! You have to move on!"

"I never want to disobey the police, but the ones causing all the trouble are being allowed to stay and destroy this man's business! People are being denied the free access of these sidewalks because of this mob! I love all of America, Officer, but the spot I love the most is the spot I'm standing on this very minute!" I told him. My son Larry had been waiting for me, and he came to my side. "Come on, son," I said to him. "We'll move, but we're going to move down *that* sidewalk!" I pointed ahead to where the pickets were packed so thick they seemed impenetrable. They pressed back and let us through, but as we passed through them it came from all sides: "We're gonna get you next, Maddox!" "We're gonna get you good!"

We walked on back to the car and drove out Hemphill Avenue to the Pickrick. As we pulled into the parking lot I still could not believe the things I had seen and heard.

"You go on in," I said to my son. "I'll be along in a minute."

As Larry walked away I thought back to the days when he was a baby. There was no Pickrick then. The ground he walked on, so firm beneath his feet, had been nothing more than a hole where people dumped their trash. That was years ago, tens of thousands of working hours in the past, and the firm ground and the building and the business that stood here now were no accident. They were the tangible proof of the opportunity that every American had, the opportunity guaranteed under the Constitution.

I had just seen a mob trampling on Charlie Leb's constitutional rights, while the police stood by and watched. I decided then and there that it would not happen to me, not the way it happened to Mr. Leb. If the police would not do their duty and protect my property and my business from these revolutionaries and bums, then they left me no choice but to protect it myself, and this I fully intended doing with every bit of strength at my disposal. I had never fired a pistol in my life, but the next day I went to a gun shop and bought a revolver, which I kept handy in my office, car, home, or wherever I felt I might need it to protect my constitutional rights.

The threats against me were not carried out immediately. After John Kennedy was assassinated in November 1963, and Lyndon Johnson ascended to the presidency, I had held out a faint hope that some sense of conservatism would find its way into the socialistic programs that had flourished under Kennedy and his liberal disciples. After all, it had been Johnson who said; "This civil rights program about which you hear so much, is nothing but a farce and a sham, an effort in the guise of liberty that would set up a police state."

But what small hope there might have been was quickly dashed as the giveaway programs of Johnson's socialistic Great Society began gnawing away at the freedoms of America which were already dissolving far too rapidly.

In Atlanta, lunch counter sit-ins began, culminating in the incredible sacking of Leb's Restaurant, and in the spring the first attempt on the Pickrick came. I believed then, as I do now, that it was my right under the Constitution to serve whomever I chose to serve in my place of business. I am a segregationist and I chose to operate my restaurant on a segregated basis. Because of this I was called a racist, although the words are far from synonymous. A segregationist is an individual—black, white, or any other color—who has enough racial pride and racial integrity and love for his fellow human beings to want to see *all* races protected and preserved.

The first attempt to violate my right to operate my restaurant as a segregated business came following the lunch rush. I had waited —as was my custom—for the majority of our patrons to finish their meal, after which Virginia and I had seated ourselves at a table to have our own lunch. I had just picked up my napkin when three whites and four blacks came dashing into the restaurant. I met them before they were ten feet inside the door, spun the first

one around, and almost had him out the door when he decided to
go limp and sit down on the floor.

I had one down, but there were six more and I called out for
help from my employees. "We got some trouble up here! I need a
little help!"

Half a dozen or so of my Negro cooks and bakers came running
from the kitchen as I attempted to drag the limp rascal toward the
door.

"These people are here to make trouble!" I said. "They're
jeopardizing my business and your jobs, and I'm paying ten dollars
for every one of them thrown out in the next ten seconds!"

The would-be troublemakers were all out on the asphalt well
before the deadline, and I doubled the payment I had promised my
employees for their prompt action. Not long after the would-be
troublemakers had driven away, an Atlanta police car pulled up at
my front door. "We got a report there's been some trouble here,
Mr. Maddox," one of the officers said.

"No, sir, there's no trouble at the Pickrick!" I told him. "There
were a few trouble *makers* here a while ago, but we've already sent
them on their way!"

The policeman nodded. "Fine. Rather you took care of it than
us."

I sensed what he meant, being under the orders of the liberal
city hall crowd who had shown their determination to sacrifice the
rights of honest, hard-working citizens to the demands of the mob.

For the next two months there were no efforts made to violate
the rules by which I ran my business, although the tension never
let up. It is a frightening thing to have a threat of this sort hanging
over you, jeopardizing everything you have spent your life working
for, knowing that when it comes you can only expect the police to
direct traffic around it while the rabble does whatever is their will.
I received numerous threats by telephone, which only served to
make me more determined to protect my own rights. The men who
framed our Constitution had to fight for their freedom, and I was
ready to fight for mine.

The civil rights bill of Johnson's Great Society was being readied
in Washington, and despite the pressure of the conservatives of
America to turn the President back onto the paths that had taken

him to his pinnacle of power, it was evident that the forces taking him in the opposite direction were greater, and he was pushing for the legislation which he had previously said would make a police state of our country.

The bill was rammed through the Congress and on July 3, 1964, Lyndon Johnson signed it into law. It was on that very afternoon that my manager, Roy Duncan, called me at home from the Pickrick.

"There were four black men here who wanted to know where you were," Duncan said. "I told them you usually went home between the noon and evening meals, but they said you were just running from them and they'd be back later."

"I hope you told them that I'm always there by five-thirty."

"Yes, sir, I did. And they said they'd be here too."

"All right, Mr. Duncan, I'll be there as soon as I can."

I put the phone down. I told Virginia what Duncan had said. "I think you'd better stay here, honey," I added.

In her quiet, determined way she simply shook her head. "No, Lester, I'm going with you."

By the time we arrived at the Pickrick it was apparent that the word was out. A large crowd was milling about, sprinkled abundantly with reporters, television cameramen, and other media representatives, which was not surprising as these agitators always alerted the media of their targets. I was hardly out of the car when they surrounded me, firing questions, poking microphones in my face, popping flashbulbs.

"What are you gonna do, Lester?"

"Do you expect trouble?"

"Will you let 'em in?"

I told them that I simply intended protecting my rights as an American citizen, with or without the help of the local police. As I worked my way through the crowd, words of encouragement came from all sides. Inside the restaurant I went into my office, where I had the revolver, and tucked it inside the belt beneath my coat and then moved back to the door to await developments.

At five-thirty sharp a car pulled into the already crowded parking lot. There were three black men inside—one of the original four had not returned—and I immediately recognized them as the "ministers" who had been ringleaders in the Leb's attack in

January, the same men who had threatened me at the time in no uncertain terms. The car pulled to a stop and the driver opened his door to get out. But I slammed the door. "You're not getting out here!"

The one sitting opposite him opened his door and climbed out, and started around the car.

"You might as well get back in there!" I told him. "You're not going to eat at the Pickrick today or any other time! This is my property, my business, and the Constitution guarantees me the right to operate it my way!"

He continued to come around toward our side. Having seen what happened at Leb's, and not knowing what he had in mind, I drew the revolver and ordered him off my property.

"Get out of here now," I said. "I have the right to protect my property and myself, and that's what I'll do!"

He looked at me, at the gun in my hand, and he turned around and got back into the car. All around us cameras were clicking and grinding away, and as the car began to pull away a cheer went up from my patrons who had come outside to see what was going on.

The photographs of Lester Maddox and his son, armed with pistol and pick handle in defense of what was theirs, were widely circulated, and everywhere the liberal press made me out a racist and bigot and rabble-rouser. I knew then, just as I know now, that I was trying to protect not only the rights of Lester Maddox, but of every citizen, including the three men I chased off my property, for if they could violate my right of private property, then there would be nothing to prevent me from violating theirs.

Strangely—or perhaps not so strangely—not one elected public official from my city, my state, or the federal government came forward to say a single word in support of my stand for my rights. I suppose they were afraid to be identified with Lester Maddox.

The incident of the afternoon was not forgotten. Out of it two suits were filed against me: one, in the state courts, on a charge of "pointing a pistol at another," the second, in federal court, was on a charge of my violating their civil rights under the new law on which Lyndon Johnson's signature had scarcely had time to dry.

There was a total absence of support of my stand for individual rights from any sector of local government. During the time that the Pickrick remained open and segregated awaiting the outcome of the two legal actions, I noticed that many government employees—federal, state, local, and even military personnel—who had been regular patrons were not showing up any more. And since the quality of the food remained at the same high level, the reason obviously had to lie somewhere else.

One of my regular customers came to me and told me his daughter was dating a young man who worked for a federal agency, and that while he had not been ordered to stay away from the Pickrick, he was well aware that it was in his best interest to do so. People such as this young man were afraid to exercise their freedom of choice, fearful that it could jeopardize their careers.

Agents of the FBI kept the Pickrick under surveillance (and subsequent integrationists who attempted to enter the Pickrick were also chaperoned by FBI agents). It became such a regular thing that we were able to recognize the individual agents, and on more than one occasion I parked behind their parked car and watched them while they watched the Pickrick. They were particularly interested in customers with out-of-state license tags on their automobiles and many of these people were harassed in strange ways. Some of them would find FBI agents waiting on their doorsteps when they reached their homes, and were questioned about their stopover in Atlanta, Georgia. One businessman from Charlotte, North Carolina, called me and related a bizarre tale of having eaten at the Pickrick with several friends, and later, heading for Connecticut on business, he was pulled over on a highway in Bluefield, West Virginia, where he was questioned on the spot by federal agents.

A man called me from Florida after undergoing unusual harassment by federal agents. Several weeks earlier he had traded cars at an Atlanta dealership. The trade-in was subsequently bought by someone who visited the Pickrick. The license number was taken down by the federal police, traced through the registration records, where the transfer had apparently not yet been made, and agents tracked the original owner down to his place of work and gave him a lengthy interrogation about why he was at the Pickrick.

"I had a hard time convincing them it wasn't me, Mr. Maddox," he said. "In fact, the whole thing is hard to believe. And you know, even if you haven't done anything, it doesn't do you any good when federal agents show your boss their badges and say they want to talk to you."

Federal agents went to college campuses, homes, places of business all over the country, tracing people who had stopped at the Pickrick and harassing them in a manner frightfully reminiscent of the police state that Lyndon Johnson himself had predicted years before in reference to the civil rights bill. It was the ultimate irony that Johnson was the man who made it a reality.

Even though many of my regular customers were intimidated to such an extent that they had to stop coming to the Pickrick, there were many new customers who came to express their support for me, and at a time when it seemed business might suffer because of the harassment by the authorities, it actually became better. Some loyal customers and supporters waited in line up to two hours to be served.

These Gestapo tactics, obviously aimed at damaging my business to the extent that I would not be able to last until the court battle, doubtless cost the United States Government—*my* government and *your* government—into the millions of dollars.

On July 8, a hearing was held in Judge Osgood Williams' court on the state charge of "pointing a pistol at another." The civil court was packed to capacity by eleven-thirty, the scheduled time of the hearing. After four hours of testimony Judge Williams bound me over to criminal court for trial, and I was realeased on $1,000 bond pending that trial. The determination of which cases are brought to trial is in the hands of the Solicitor of the Criminal Court, who at the time was John I. Kelley. Mr. Kelley was not seeking re-election to the post, and apparently he wanted nothing to do with this case and announced that it was dead, as far as he was concerned.

My own attorneys informed me that this merely meant it would not be docketed during the remainder of his term unless the plantiffs took it to the grand jury. This, in effect, postponed my trial before a jury of my peers for some nine months.

The federal charge turned out to be a different matter entirely. The NAACP joined forces with lawyers of Bobby Kennedy, which meant simply that cost was no object, and whatever was required in the way of manpower or money to press the case would be forthcoming. Witnesses, many of whom were professional agitators or dupes of the many Communist-inspired groups so active at the time, were brought in from all over the country at government expense to testify against me.

As for myself, I had two capable Atlanta attorneys, William G. McRae and Sidney Schell. Before settling on these men I had discussed my situation with numerous other lawyers and I was both amazed and disheartened at the estimates of what the costs would run through appeals up to the Supreme Court. I also got the impression that some of the larger law firms did not want to take the case at any price, fearing the unpopularity of my stand in the eyes of the courts. Perhaps they feared reprisals at the hands of these liberal courts, where their being identified with Lester Maddox might result in adverse decisions involving other clients. A law firm on retainer to a large utility has constant contact with the courts on behalf of its client, and the firm would not want to endanger this lucrative relationship for anything so unimportant as a stand for constitutional principles.

In this heavily lopsided situation of the federal government and the NAACP, with all its foundation funding, against a single individual, a move had begun to gather money for my defense. It was a true grass roots campaign, begun by ordinary people in ordinary jobs. There were airline employees, steel workers, firemen, policemen, telephone workers, people from all walks of life who were aware that their liberties were on the line just as mine were. Not only adults pitched in, but children as well. One little girl eating with her folks at the Pickrick gave me a dollar she said she had earned raking leaves. Another gave me ten dollars she got for her birthday. In all, more than $17,000 was given, and it went a long way toward helping pay my legal fees.

No time was lost in moving ahead with this case, as it was to test the constitutionality of the Civil Rights Act. The trial was set for July 17, in the Old Post Office Building in downtown Atlanta. There were two cases to be heard that morning. Moreton Rolleston, owner of the Heart of Atlanta Motel, had filed suit against the Civil Rights Act on the same day that LBJ signed it into law, claiming that integration would damage the business and the reputation of the motel. Rolleston asked $11 million in damages.

There was to be no trial by jury. Bobby Kennedy, Lyndon Johnson, and others behind the Civil Rights Act knew full well that court tests left up to a jury would almost certainly strike it down, therefore violations were considered civil rather than criminal acts, allowing for trial by judge, not jury. I will always feel that this violated my constitutional rights. Three federal judges —District Court Judges Frank Hooper and Lewis Morgan, and the Chief Judge of the Fifth Circuit Court of Appeals, Elbert Tuttle—were impaneled. The Heart of Atlanta case was heard first, with Rolleston, who was also a lawyer, arguing his own case. This took most of the morning, and my case came up after the lunch recess.

Thus, without the benefit of a jury of my peers, my trial began. The government brought out a vast array of witnesses to prove that my business was involved in interstate commerce. It was set forth in the Civil Rights Act that, for the law to apply, the defendant must be shown to serve interstate customers and that a substantial quantity of the food sold he received through interstate shipments. FBI agents gave minute testimony about the number of cars in my parking lot at various times, where they were from, who the people were. Before it was done, more than twenty witnesses had taken the stand against me.

Three days later the court handed down its opinion. It declared the Civil Rights Act to be constitutional, and also declared that it covered Lester Maddox and the Pickrick Restaurant. The forces opposing private enterprise and private property rights had won out, with the federal government showing more determination in wiping out the Pickrick than it had shown in defeating our enemies in both World Wars.

I held out faint hope that the Supreme Court would see that what was happening was clearly against the Constitution, even though the Warren court was the most liberal in the country's history, and Earl Warren had already done more to destroy our system of government than any Chief Justice before him. But this hope, faint though it was, vanished completely when I was denied a hearing. This denial came about because another case had been heard earlier, that of Ollie's Barbecue of Birmingham, Alabama. The lower court's decision that the Civil Rights Act was constitutional had been upheld. I felt then—and now—that the merits of my case were far stronger and that at least a glimmer of hope would have remained for justice being done had my case reached the Supreme Court first. Even if justice had not been dispensed, my arguments would have been heard.

Both the Pickrick and the Heart of Atlanta Motel were enjoined from refusing to serve blacks, this to become effective on August 11 to allow our lawyers sufficient time to prepare appeals or to attempt to secure a stay order from the Supreme Court.

During the interim business was excellent at the Pickrick. Well-wishers came by the hundreds. I placed a barrel of pick handles near the door, representing the "pick" in Pickrick, advertising them as souvenirs or otherwise for two dollars each, and I sat a manikin on a bench in plain view, with a knife in its back and a sign which read: "This manikin represents what has happened to the American private enterprise system."

But the prosperity of the Pickrick was to be short-lived. On August 10, Supreme Court Justice Hugo Black denied the stays of the injunction that my lawyers had applied for. The next day an effort to integrate the Pickrick had already taken place when I arrived prior to the noon meal. Two young blacks showed up at about ten-thirty and had been told by my Negro supervisor of the baking department that the restaurant was not yet open. He requested the two to leave, for if they persisted the Pickrick would close and put seventy-five people out of work.

A large group of my supporters was on hand when I got there. When I was advised of what had happened I told the crowd, "We are never going to integrate! The Pickrick belongs to Lester Maddox, not to Lyndon Johnson or the news media or the agitators or Nikita Khrushchev!"

The two blacks had gone, but a car carrying five more pulled into the parking lot as we began serving the noon meal. Four of them got out and headed for the front door, where one of my sons met them. I joined him the moment I heard what was happening. This was a showdown and I was well aware of it. I could not legally turn them away as this was the date set forth in the federal injunction.

I stood in the doorway and spoke to them. "I ask you to leave. My position is clear; I am not going to serve people other than those of my choice, and if you insist on trying to come in, I'll have to close and dismiss my employees, both black and white."

Inside, customers had gotten up from their tables and pressed toward the door behind us. Photographers, reporters, television people—who were always on hand for these efforts—swarmed in from all sides. The crush was so great that even if I had allowed the four agitators access, I doubt that they could have physically gotten in.

This was still the situation when our normal two-thirty closing time came. The four got back into the waiting car after informing reporters that they would be back when we reopened at five.

The news of this brought hundreds of people to Hemphill Avenue long before the five o'clock deadline. When Virginia and I arrived from home we were startled to find that the police had blocked off the entire street in front of the restaurant and at the ends of the block to the north and south all traffic was being routed around our place of business.

"What are you doing?" I asked the first officer I found.

"We've got orders to direct traffic around your place."

"But you can't keep my customers away!"

The officer shrugged. "Don't talk to me, Mr. Maddox. I just work here. You'll have to talk to the captain."

I located the officer in charge. "My place is open and ready for business and you're preventing my customers from passing! I demand that you lift this roadblock!"

He assured me that his men would let my customers through—which I later learned was not the case at all—and that he had orders to divert the traffic away from my business and he intended to carry out his orders.

"Is the Justice Department running the Atlanta Police now!"

"Orders, Mr. Maddox," he said, and walked away.

"The police state has come to Atlanta!" I said to the throng around me. "This is the worst thing that has ever happened in this country! The Atlanta Police are doing more to put me out of business than the Communists, the racial agitators, and the federal government combined!"

I was not going to take it lying down. I ran to the parking lot, where I had a brief talk with Virginia and with my daughter

Ginny. We each got into a car. I drove to Eighth Street, where the roadblock was diverting traffic off Hemphill, and I parked my car crosswise in the middle of the street, got out, and locked the car. Virginia did the same at Clayton Street and Ginny on Ponders Avenue. Traffic in all directions came to an immediate halt. There was nowhere to go with all the streets blocked off.

"You can't leave your car there!" a police officer told me. "Get it outta there!"

"I'll be glad to move it as soon as the Atlanta Police remove the roadblock in front of the Pickrick!" I replied.

"We'll have to tow it away if you won't move it voluntarily!"

"Then call the wrecker!"

Transit buses were being allowed to pass the roadblock, and I hopped on the first one to come by and rode down to the opposite intersection, where the police were blockading the Pickrick. Virginia and Ginny had done as I instructed them, but in a few minutes I saw the red blinkers down the way as the wreckers arrived. I hurried to Virginia's car, where one of the wreckers was already in position to hook on. People were talking to the driver, and when he saw me he said, "Is this your car, Mr. Maddox?"

"Yes, sir, it is! And that's right where I want it to stay!"

"Well, if that's where you want it, that's where it stays!" He got out and, climbing up on top of the cab, he sat down and looked around at the crowd. "Yes, sir, they can have my job before I'll move a car of Lester Maddox!"

A second wrecker was brought up and as soon as it came to a stop I reached in and removed the ignition key. However, when the driver, a black man, recognized me, he said he would have no part of moving my car if I didn't want it moved. I shook his hand, gave him back his keys and two one-dollar bills, and he drove off.

The police had called every wrecker service in the city, and, unable to get any to accept the job, called in a police wrecker. By the time this was done, however, the crowd had swollen to such large proportions that the wrecker was unable to get through the mass of people to hook onto the car.

I knew the rank and file of the Police Department did not relish this work. They supported my views, but they had their orders and they had to carry them out. The situation was becoming serious for the police. The people did not look kindly on this violation of a

14. As governor in 1969, with late Speaker of the Georgia House of Representatives George L. Smith and Lieutenant Governor George T. Smith. (Photo by Bob Connell)

15. En route to Governors Conference in Williamsburg, Virginia. That's newsman Bill Buckner with his back to the camera, and behind me and Virginia are Mr. and Mrs. J. L. Allen.

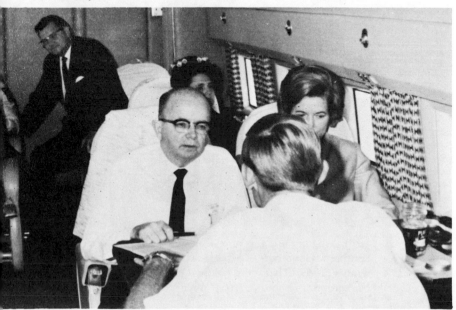

16. Taking in the sights on my bicycle before the start of the Southern Governors Conference in Williamsburg in September 1969. That's the colonial magazine arsenal in the background. (Photo courtesy Wide World Photos)

17. In the hospital in Atlanta, awaiting surgery for removal of a kidney stone in June 1970. (Photo courtesy Wide World Photos)

18. Relaxing on deck at the National Governors Conference in Osage Beach, Missouri, August 1970. (Photo courtesy Wide World Photos)

man's right to operate his business, and they did not like being prevented from eating at the Pickrick if they chose to do so. In short, the police had created a condition that could rapidly deteriorate, and one of the captains in charge came to me with a proposition.

"Pickrick," he said (most of them did not know my name, and called me that), "if we can get the superintendent to open up Hemphill Avenue, will you help disperse this crowd and move your cars?"

"Yes, sir," I replied. "I wouldn't have had the cars there and this crowd wouldn't be here to start with if you people hadn't tried to destroy my rights and my business. Let's go see the superintendent!"

I told the superintendent exactly what I had told the captain. He agreed to remove the blockade and as soon as that was done and traffic began to flow on Hemphill Avenue, the crowd dispersed of its own accord. As to whether the agitators who had announced they would be there ever showed up, I have no knowledge. I know I did not see them.

On August 13, I was served with an order from Judge Hooper to show cause why I should not be held in contempt of court for allegedly refusing service to the four blacks at the noon meal. On the same day, a pair of racial agitators accompanied by two agents of the FBI, walked into the Pickrick. This was it. I blocked their way, and looking at the two agitators, I said, "You sorry, no-good Communists. You have just put sixty-six people out of work. You've stolen my business. The Pickrick is closed. Now get out of here!"

My restaurant remained closed for the next month and a half. I kept all my employees on the payroll during this time, and although I sold souvenirs, I sustained a net loss during this time of more than $50,000.

The Pickrick was a corporation, of which Lester Maddox was the agent. Conferring with my lawyers it was decided that the corporation could lease the restaurant to Lester Maddox as an individual, and this was done. The Lester Maddox Cafeteria was opened and my faithful patrons and supporters streamed in. I was quickly hailed back into court, where this was labeled a "subterfuge" and I was ordered to accept every customer regardless of race, color, or national origin. If I did not comply, a fine of $200 a day would be levied against me, and this would be retroactive to the day of the order.

This immediately brought an outpouring of offers from my friends and supporters. Scores of people came to me and offered to mail me a dollar a day to help pay the fine. I had to refuse. Whether I agreed with the court or not, I did not want to stand in contempt.

My stand had been costly. My savings were gone by this time, and only the daily patronage of hundreds of faithful customers kept me from going under financially. A decision had to be made now, because this was without any doubt the end of the line. I met in private on the next Saturday morning with my accountant Herbert Cheek, and my two attorneys, Sidney Schell and William McRae.

"You've done everything you could do, Lester," they told me. "You have to comply now, or everything you've got will go down the drain."

I argued that I could not give up the stand I knew was right. But after nearly three hours of discussion, during which time I weighed the loss to my family and to the employees who had remained so loyal to me throughout these trying times, I reluctantly agreed. Together we drew up a statement of surrender; I would bow down to the police state.

Members of the news media were always on hand during this time, and I called them together in one of the dining rooms and made my announcement. When they had rushed off to get their stories in I sat there alone, feeling broken and almost as if life itself had vanished. My son Lester, Jr., came in, a bewildered look on his face.

"Dad . . . I don't understand. You told me you wouldn't ever give up."

I looked up at the boy, recalling that I had promised him this. In my decision to give up I had thought it would be the best thing for Virginia and the children, that a man had to sacrifice his beliefs and convictions when they were in conflict with his family's welfare. Now, as my son stood waiting for an explanation which I could not give him, I knew that my decision had been wrong. At that moment, he gave me the necessary strength and courage to do what I should have done all along.

I felt as though a massive weight had suddenly been lifted off my shoulders. "Son, I did tell you that, didn't I? I made a commitment to you because of my convictions." I stood up. "And your daddy is going to stand by his promise to you!"

The following day, Sunday, a Negro man appeared at the door at the usual hour of opening. I had prepared a simple sign for the inevitable occasion, and now I turned, closed the door of the business I had painstakingly built over a period of two decades, and hung the sign on the door. It read: CLOSED.

It was a sad and tragic moment, not merely for Lester Maddox, but for every American citizen. The sign was symbolic of the door that had been closed to individual opportunity and private property rights all over this land.

Chapter 6

Maddox Country—The Race for Governor: 1966

In 1961, after I lost the Atlanta mayoral race to Ivan Allen, a newsman asked me about my plans for the future. I told him I just might run for governor. Three years later, during the long, hot summer when the federal government was taking away both my liberty and my business (and I was only one of millions), an old friend, Courtney Wynne, remarked to me: "Lester, this thing will make you governor."

I was fighting for what I believed to be right. I was far too busy trying to protect my rights at the time to think of running for anything, but I knew full well if Courtney's remark had any validity to it, it would only be because the voters felt my struggle was right.

I have been asked innumerable times: "Why didn't you comply with the law and keep the Pickrick open? What would have been the harm?"

What would have been the harm if those patriots had not tossed the tea into Boston Harbor? What would have been the harm if we had simply rebuilt Pearl Harbor after the Japanese flew away? It was simply that I was not going to knuckle under to a law that I believed went against the basic precepts of freedom as set forth in the Constitution, and so I shut down my business rather than violate a law I felt was unjust, as many were doing in the so-called civil rights movement.

A lease of the restaurant to some former employees did not work out, and I later sold the property to Georgia Tech and it became a part of that campus.

Standing up for one's beliefs is one thing; making a living for one's family is another. The following summer I opened a retail furniture store, keeping my established name, Pickrick. But in the interim I had been giving increasingly serious consideration to getting into the 1966 race for governor. The same month the Pickrick Furniture Store opened for business—September 1965—I announced that I was a candidate. It was twelve months before the Democratic primary, but I felt I could not wait to see which way the political winds would be blowing.

To say that my candidacy was not taken seriously by the breed referred to as "political observers" would be a monumental understatement. To them I was a three-time loser. If they took note of it at all, it must have seemed absurd—after running twice for mayor of Atlanta and once for lieutenant governor of Georgia, without a win—for Lester Maddox to be announcing his candidacy for governor.

I looked at it differently. I had started low, and worked my way up.

The campaign got off to a slow start. Virginia undertook the operation of the store, as she had done with the Pickrick in past campaigns. There was the ever present problem of money. As if to compound the usual troubles, I was hospitalized in the late fall for surgery, and although the operation itself was not of a particularly serious nature, there developed unforeseen complications which left me in poor physical condition for many weeks. There were times when I felt I could scarcely climb the curb after crossing a street, and yet, even with these foreboding beginnings, I never doubted that I would be the next governor of Georgia. This was not conceit on my part, as it might appear to some, nor was it blind faith resulting from political naïveté. It was simply something I *knew* in my heart.

As my health slowly returned, I began to move about the state. Two friends, J. L. Allen and Buster Sutton, both of whom had helped me in my earlier campaigns, volunteered their assistance as drivers when they could get away, and before the campaign was done we had traveled more than 100,000 miles over Georgia's highways and byways. It was, as usual, a shoestring campaign. Most candidates in that race seemed to be well financed, and, apparently on the assumption that I fell into that category, a gentleman in the outdoor advertising business came to me one day.

"Mr. Maddox," he said, "I'd like to help you get elected."

"Well, sir," I replied truthfully, "I can sure use all the help I can get."

"Billboards. That's what you need! Big billboards with your picture on them, from the Tennessee line to Florida, from Alabama to the Atlantic Ocean. We can do the job for you for only $96,000!"

I had to laugh. "Sir, I appreciate your offer, but to tell you the truth, if you had said $960, I still couldn't do it."

To make up for the lack of billboards, I had fifty thousand posters printed, at a cost of slightly over two cents apiece, half of them reading MADDOX WITHOUT A RUNOFF; the other half, THIS IS MADDOX COUNTRY. I would fill the station wagon with these posters, copies of my platform, bubble gum, boxes of small American flags, and other campaign material, and before dawn be on the road, sometimes with Buster or J.L. driving, sometimes alone. All along the way the posters would be tacked up on trees, poles, and if I happened onto one of the big expensive billboards proclaiming the desirability of one of my opponents, six or eight MADDOX COUNTRY posters would go up in the immediate vicinity. If Buster or J.L. happened to be driving, they would pull the car up to whatever the poster was going on, I would climb up on the hood, reach as high as I could, and hammer one up. Later I carried a ladder on top of the station wagon for this purpose, as the supporters of my opponents had a bad habit of pulling down my posters if they were within easy reach.

Virginia went along with me from time to time. I recall we were driving to Statesboro one night. It was about 2:00 A.M. and when I would get out and tack up a poster the sound of the hammer would set dogs barking and chickens cackling at the nearby farmhouses. I stopped this late night activity for fear I was waking up too many people.

At a Georgia Forestry Commission breakfast, one of the officials told me, "When you have the time, I'd like to take you out to see some of our Georgia forest lands."

"I appreciate the offer," I replied, "but I've tacked Maddox signs on more Georgia pines then most people have ever seen!"

We went into scores of small towns absolutely cold, with no advance work of any sort. We parked the station wagon and walked around the square or business section. I shook hands with everyone, introduced myself, gave them some campaign literature, and gave the kids bubble gum and a flag.

In the early months of 1966, the candidates referred to by the media as "serious" began to toss in their hats. Lester Maddox, as a candidate, was still looked down upon by most of the state's daily newspapers—especially the Cox monopoly in Atlanta—as well as most major radio and television stations around Georgia, as something of a joke. The opinion makers were saying this was going to be the first real two-party race in modern Georgia history, and that we would see Ernest Vandiver, a former Democratic governor, or wealthy young Republican congressman and textile heir, Howard "Bo" Callaway, in the statehouse in 1967.

This situation underwent an unexpected change in the late spring. Vandiver, who had suffered a heart attack during his 1959–63 term as governor, was advised by his doctors that the continued stress and strain of a hotly fought political battle could endanger his health and possibly his life. A politician can argue with a lot of things, but not with his own doctors, and Ernest Vandiver reluctantly announced his withdrawal from the race.

Politics, like nature, abhors a vacuum. The vacuum in the gubernatorial race was particularly strong. For a few days it even seemed that Senator Herman Talmadge himself might enter the race, but neither the people of Georgia nor the powers of the party looked favorably on the loss of seniority in Washington, and Talmadge stayed where he was. That triggered the real scramble. Comptroller General Jimmy Bentley and Agriculture Commissioner Phil Campbell weighed their chances and decided the time was not right. Former Lieutenant Governor Garland Byrd, State Senator Jimmy Carter, and James Gray, a newspaper publisher and television station owner from Albany in south Georgia, apparently felt differently about their chances and tossed their hats in. These—added to those already running, Ellis Arnall, Hoke O'Kelley, and Lester Maddox—made a field of six Democrats, which virtually assured a runoff, as a majority of the vote was required to nominate. From the September 14 primary, the two top vote-getters (assuming there was no majority) would go into the runoff, and the victor emerging from that would then take on "Bo" Callaway, who had been chosen in convention rather than by primary election.

With Vandiver out, the major pools showed Arnall to be front-runner. Some other—and less widely recognized—polls came up with a different picture. The Smitty's Barbershop poll, in Smyrna, Georgia, for example, showed Lester Maddox in the lead by a comfortable margin.

It was not until well into the summer that my candidacy really began to be taken seriously by some observers. A United Press International political analyst wrote in July: "Lester Maddox entered the governor's race and everyone said 'Ha ha.' Now nobody's laughing."

From the first time I had gotten into a political race I had been absolutely determined that I would not create any debts along the way that would have to be paid off by political favoritism. However, I did attempt to convince a number of key political figures that Lester Maddox was not going to be an also-ran in this race, and that the sooner they recognized this as fact, the better. One of these was Jim Gillis, the longtime state highway commissioner, a man of great political power. At the time Ernest Vandiver was still a candidate, "Mr. Jim," as he was called, backed the former governor. My only direct contact with him had been years before, as a private citizen, when Highway 41 had been rerouted from in front of the Pickrick. I phoned him and told him who I was. "I'd like to talk to you about putting your support behind the winning candidate. I'm going to be the next governor of Georgia and if you aren't with me now, you will be before it's over."

If he was surprised at the call, his voice didn't show it. "We're not against you, Mr. Maddox," he said. "We like you, and we appreciate the position you stand for. But some of the fellas say you're just too hardheaded."

"Well, Mr. Jim," I said, "the fellas may be right about my being hardheaded if they mean I'll stick by what I believe is right, but they're gonna have to decide whether they want a hardheaded Democrat or a Republican."

We talked for quite some time, but it was apparent to me that the established political structure was too set and unyielding to let in an outsider who had not come by the traditionally accepted route. When Vandiver announced his withdrawal from the race shortly after this, Gillis and other top figures in the state's Democratic Party looked around for another candidate to support. Ellis

Arnall was an avowed national Democrat, and they were unable to accept the implied liberalism that went along with that. I doubt if any consideration whatever was given to Lester Maddox; James Gray, former state party chairman, was given the nod.

I still had the Democratic Party opposing me, while the daily media not only opposed me but conducted a virtual smear campaign. News stories—so-called—as well as editorials and cartoons were slanted to make Lester Maddox out as some sort of throwback to the dark ages, a racist, bigot, hatemonger. They made no attempt to discern the truth, to examine my published platform, which was more progressive than that of any of the other candidates. One of the things that drew me into politics was my observation of candidates promising the moon simply to gain office, while ignoring all their promises once they were in. I fully intended doing everything I could to implement mine. I am convinced that it was this camapign by the media against me that caused the race eventually to go into a runoff. I have never sought the support of the media, but I believe that fair treatment is not too much to ask, not just for myself, but for the people of Georgia. All too often the guarantees of the First Amendment under which they operate are not only exercised, they are abused.

I have always known where to go to find my support, and my Pontiac station wagon continued to take me there—to the people. As the September primary drew nearer, my growing support with the rank-and-file citizen became a serious concern of some of my opponents, and prompted one of the most bizarre efforts I have ever seen in any campaign.

Several days before the September 14 Democratic primary, a distant relative, whom I shall refer to as "Bud," came to see me at my home in Atlanta. He told me that a strange thing had happened on a flight from Atlanta to his home in Texas. Three men had struck up a conversation with him, and it quickly became obvious that it had not simply been a casual thing. They knew he was related to me and they asked him to relay a message to me.

"They are interested in seeing another candidate elected, and they feel that you being in the race is interfering with his chances. They said it would be worth a lot to them if you would consider withdrawing on some pretext like ill health."

I was amazed, and more than a little incredulous. "What did they mean about it being worth a lot to them?"

"Well, Lester, they said maybe $250,000."

I laughed. "It's just some kind of joke, Bud!"

"No," he said quickly. "It's no joke. They said a candidate dropped out of another statewide race a few years ago, that he was paid $100,000 for saying his health was bad."

There was definitely something peculiar about this. "Do you know who they are? Or who the candidate is? I don't see how anybody would be willing to spend that kind of money to get a man out of the race!"

"I don't know who it is," Bud said. "But think about this, Lester. Anybody that'd pay a quarter of a million dollars to a man to get him out of the race, do you think they wouldn't pay somebody five thousand dollars to get rid of him permanently if he didn't take their offer."

The thought had already crossed my mind. Of course, I had absolutely no idea of taking such a bribe, but I told Bud I wanted to find out more about it, and he left, saying he would contact me in a few days.

He phoned me two days later. "These people are ready to go, Lester. They want to know when they can meet with you."

"I don't have any idea when we can meet. I've got to go to Macon this morning to address a luncheon meeting."

"They want to meet you today. You'll have to cancel the Macon deal."

"I'm not about to cancel out!"

There was a pause, and I sensed that he was passing this information on to someone else. Then he said, "All right. They'll meet you in Macon."

By this time I was convinced that whoever it was meant business, and I felt that it had gone far enough, that I would do well to break it off entirely. But the thought occurred to me that I should expose them. I would report what had happened to the authorities and catch them in the act of trying to buy me out of the race.

"All right, Bud. I'm to address a civic group at the S&S Cafeteria at noon, and then I'm going to the Dempsey Hotel. I'll be registered there."

"That's good, Lester," he said, and hung up.

J. L. Allen went on this trip with me and during the ninety-odd mile drive to Macon I told him the whole story. J.L. was as incredulous as I had been. When we reached the Macon city limits I told him to pull into a service station, where I phoned the local office of the FBI and told them I would like to meet with an agent in regard to an attempted bribe.

Two agents met us downtown and I went over the whole story with them.

"It's an interesting story, Mr. Maddox," one of them said when I had finished, "but there is nothing in the way of a violation of federal law involved in this. Maybe you should talk to the local police."

J.L. and I drove then to police headquarters, where I asked for the chief of detectives. I was advised that he was having an early lunch at a nearby restaurant, and we hurried there, where I found him in the foyer. I introduced myself and again repeated the story. When I was done he looked at me for a moment. "I don't believe that, Maddox," he said flatly. "Who the devil would give *you* that kind of money just to get you out of the race?"

Apparently he felt that I had no chance of winning and why would anyone give me fifteen cents to get out or to stay in?

"Why don't you get yourself a lawyer?" he said, and turned and walked back to his table.

I made a final effort by going to the courthouse and repeating the story to a county official, only to get the same response I had gotten from the FBI, that it was not a matter that came under their jurisdiction.

I went to the luncheon for my speaking engagement and when that was over we drove to the Dempsey and checked in. I knew there was no way I would go through with the offer, and now that I had been turned down by law enforcement authorities, I did not know where to turn. As J.L. and I walked across the lobby toward the elevator, I saw a reporter I knew, Sam Hopkins of the Atlanta *Constitution,* in the company of a Macon newspaperman. Even though Hopkins' paper was solidly against me, this was a news story and I accosted him and once again related the tale from the beginning.

"All I ask you is that you try to listen outside my room when they come there with the money," I told him.

Whether they believed me or not, I do not know. They did agree to wait and see what developed. I told J.L. to stay down in the lobby and I would call him when contact was made, and then I went up to the room, 519.

I had been there only a few minutes when there was a knock at the door. It was Bud. "They're ready, Lester," he said. "They want you to come down the hall to their room." He reached inside his jacket and brought out a paper. "All you have to do is sign this and the money's yours."

I took the paper. It was a letter addressed to George Stewart, Secretary of the Georgia Democratic Party, and it read:

> Due to my physical condition it would be both impossible and unwise for me to complete my campaign for Governor of Georgia and, therefore, this is my formal notification to you that I am withdrawing from the Democratic Primary election for the Governorship. I would appreciate your returning my $2500 qualification fee at your convenience.

I looked up at Bud. "What's their room number? I'll come there as soon as I shave."

It was obvious that he did not want to go without me, but he gave me the number and I let him out. At the door he paused. "Don't be long, Lester."

When he was gone I folded the letter and stuffed it down inside one of my socks, then I picked up the phone and called J.L. in the lobby. "Get Sam Hopkins and that other reporter. I'll wait a few minutes to give you time to get up here." I told him the number of the room where I was to meet with them, and when I figured they had had time to get to the fifth floor I left my room and walked down the corridor and knocked on their door. I saw J.L. with the two reporters waiting down the corridor. The door opened and I stepped inside.

"Good to see you, Mr. Maddox." The man who spoke was seated in a chair. Bud had opened the door for me, and two other men stood near the twin beds opposite the door.

"They've got the money, Lester," Bud said. "They're ready to pay you."

I figured that J.L. and the reporters should be outside the door by this time, and I said, rather loudly, "Let's see the money."

One of them reached quickly beneath the bed and pulled out a suitcase, which he laid on the bed and opened. Inside were seven large packets of tightly strapped bills. The two men took the bundles out of the suitcase and placed them on my outstretched hands and arms. Three of the bundles were twenty-dollar bills, each with the figure $20,000 written on the wrapper. The other four were tens, each containing $10,000.

I looked at it. "Good gracious!" I said, "that's the most money I've ever seen in my whole life!" I hoped those outside the door had heard me, and I gazed down at all that money for a few moments, not caring that it was $100,000 and not the $250,000 Bud had originally mentioned. It would not have made any difference to me if it had been a million. I thought of the lean months behind me, of how I had been campaigning for more than seven months before the total contributions had even reached one thousand dollars. I thought of all the people, young and old, who had shared their meager earnings with me, many of them constricted by fixed incomes, but who somehow managed one dollar, or five or ten, because they believed in the cause I represented. I remembered a young girl who wrote me, enclosing a dollar bill which she said was half of the first money she had earned as a babysitter. The other dollar, she wrote, was for herself and the Lord's work.

I threw the money forward onto the bed, and the fellow in the chair jumped up. "What's the matter!"

"Man, I don't want that stuff!"

Bud took a step toward me, a look of shock on his face. "What do you mean, Lester? There's nothing wrong! You're an honorable man and they're all honorable men! There's nothing wrong with this!"

"I think I'm an honorable man," I said. "And that's why I'm not taking that money."

The man who had been seated, obviously the one in charge, glanced at Bud and the others. "You all take the money and go on out. I want to talk to Lester."

One of the others shook his head. "We'll wait outside but let's leave the money here."

The man in charge agreed and the others left the room. He looked at me for several moments and then he said, "We know this campaign's put you in debt—"

I laughed. "I've got $4,200 in printing bills right now that I don't know how I'm gonna pay!"

"And you've got a wife and two kids at home—"

I interrupted him again. "A wife and four children."

He nodded and went on. "You can take that hundred thousand and head right back up the Atlanta road with it. It's tax-free, you can pay off your debts and you and your family can live good."

"Sir, do you know that the income and savings and investments I've lost by standing up for what I believe in would exceed half a million dollars? Do you think I would back away now and betray the confidence of the people who support me for a hundred thousand? Why, you could fill up this room with money and it wouldn't be enough to make me do that!"

I turned and left the room. I walked past Bud and the others who were standing in the corridor and went back to my room. Less than a minute later Bud knocked on the door and asked me for the letter he had given me to sign.

"I don't know where it is. I must have misplaced it."

He glanced around the room for a moment, then hurried out. A short time later I stepped into the corridor. There was no sign of Bud or his companions, but J. L. Allen, Sam Hopkins, and the Macon reporter were walking toward me. They said they had not been able to hear everything that was said in the room, but they had heard me exclaim about the money. I told them the rest of it and the newsmen hurried off to file the story.

We continued the Macon schedule and then went back to the Dempsey Hotel to freshen up before driving south for the following day's engagements. I found out later that the men who were in the hotel room had picked up $150,000 at a downtown Atlanta bank, had hurriedly counted it, packed it in the suitcase, and had barely had time to get to Macon to meet me. They must have been mighty disappointed when I tossed that money on the bed, because they were going to divide the $50,000 that they held back, their cut for getting the job done.

As we were preparing to leave at about four o'clock that afternoon, my younger brother, Wesley, arrived at the hotel. I was surprised to see him, and I asked him what he was doing in Macon, that I thought he would be working at campaign headquarters in Atlanta.

"That's where I was going when I heard the news on the radio about the attempt to bribe you out of the race. I talked it over with Joyce and some others at campaign headquarters, and we decided it would be a good idea for me to come down here and ride the rest of the way with you and J.L."

I did not believe I needed bodyguards, but under the circumstances I was not sorry to have Wesley along. As we all got into the station wagon, Wesley told J.L. to stop down the block where he had parked his car. He opened the trunk and came back carrying a shotgun.

"That's a long road to Bainbridge, Lester," he said, "and your itinerary's no secret. It won't hurt to have this along."

"All right, Wesley," I said. J.L. headed the car out of Macon and I leaned back and closed my eyes. I was asleep before we reached the city limits.

The final days of the primary campaign went without further incident of that sort, which led me to believe it was not a direct effort of one of my opponents, but more likely a misguided and unauthorized attempt by overzealous supporters of one or more of them. Whoever it was had misjudged Lester Maddox badly, but they had assessed my strength correctly. The voters went to the polls on September 13. Former Governor Ellis Arnall, as predicted, led the pack with some 231,000 votes. Lester Maddox followed with nearly 186,000, with the other candidates bringing up the rear.

It was Arnall and Maddox in a runoff, my third in four political races, and although I had been hopeful in the others, I had a strong feeling now that this was it, that victory was a virtual certainty.

After the primary, and prior to the runoffs, an old friend, Jack Gunter, had brought a young man to meet me. His name was Tommy Irvin, a state legislator from Habersham County in the northern part of the state. Tall, affable, quick-witted, and a consummate politician, Irvin told me he had been taking note of an increasingly obvious fact during his own re-election campaign.

"The boys in the courthouses aren't for you, Mr. Maddox, but I don't suppose that's news to you. But it's a different story when I'm out talking to the people. The way I see it, you're going to be the next governor of Georgia, and I'd like to help you get there."

Throughout the years, not only in this campaign, I had been wary of accepting support from any political figure on anything but my own ground rules. I had seen too much of the disastrous results of favoritism and cronyism in government. I made my position on this clear, thanked him, and accepted his offer of support. He had already won the Democratic primary, and there being no opposition to him in the general election, he immediately became active in my runoff campaign.

Some time later, when I was absolutely certain of his sincerity, I asked him, "Tommy, what do you want when I'm governor?"

"Nothing, Lester," he said. "I just want you to be the best governor this state ever had."

"I don't know if I can be the best, but I've sure got to be better than average. If I'm not, I'll go down in history as the worst, my critics will see to that."

It was not long before these critics were screaming their heads off. The primary runoff was slated for September 28, and most predictions were that it was going to be close. When the polls had closed on the twenty-eighth, Maddox headquarters at the Henry Grady Hotel was packed as the first returns began to come in. From the very beginning it was obvious that the predictions were sadly mistaken, and by ten that night I had taken such a commanding lead that Mr. Arnall conceded his defeat.

Even before my nomination was made official, some of the liberals were behaving as if the end of the world had just been confirmed. They had been calling me so many things for so long that they had brainwashed themselves into believing beyond a doubt that it was all true, that the image they had created of Lester Maddox, the caricature, was the real Lester Maddox. The statement made by Atlanta Mayor Ivan Allen on the morning of the twenty-ninth summed up the hatred of the whole pack:

> It is deplorable that the combined forces of ignorance, prejudice, reactionism and the duplicity of many Republican voters have thrust upon the State of Georgia

Lester Maddox, a totally unqualified individual, as the Democratic nominee for governor. The seal of the great State of Georgia lies tarnished. The wisdom, justice and moderation espoused by our founding fathers must not be surrendered to the rabble of prejudice, extremism, buffoonery, and incompetence.

It is strange logic indeed that causes a man to look upon his own winning of an election as an infallible sign of intelligence and deep wisdom on the part of the voting public, while another man's victory at the same polls reflects only the voters' incapability of handling matters which were, incidentally, entrusted to them by our founding fathers.

Mayor Allen's violent opposition, in the long run, gave me a boost at the polls, and I could only feel sorry for a man who became so obsessed with hatred that his actions more closely resembled those of a spoiled child than of the chief executive of a great city. Unwittingly he provided a turning point in my campaign, for the thousands of Georgians who saw and heard this mindless fury being vented, realized that it was really their intelligence and integrity that were under attack. In south Georgia, people came up to me and said, "You know, I hadn't made up my mind until I heard what Ivan Allen was saying. I'm voting for you now!"

In any event, I had no time to waste in listening to the outpouring of vitriol from this element. An overwhelming majority had picked me to be the Democratic standard-bearer, and I now had to go after Mr. Howard "Bo" Callaway.

Chapter 7

From Chief Cook to Chief Executive

If some of the calls and visitors I received the day after my runoff victory in the primary provided any yardstick, I had been the most elusive individual in the entire state of Georgia. Politicians from across the state—most of whom had never before spoken to me—were treating me like a long lost brother. "Lester!" it would begin. "Man, you are *hard* to find! I been trying to get ahold of you for six months or more! We been planning a big barbecue for you next time you're down in our county!"

The primary had been rough on the Georgia Democratic Party, there was no doubt about that, and while I made it very clear that candidate Lester Maddox was going to incur no political indebtedness that Governor Lester Maddox would have to pay off, I was the party nominee and I had to do everything I could to hold the party together. One of my recent opponents, James Gray, had been Democratic chairman a few years earlier and I had talked to him many months ago—prior to his entering the race—about resuming that post after my nomination. He was an able administrator and fund raiser, and he accepted the appointment. I also sought the support and backing of as many of my recent opponents as possible.

During the long, hot summer, while the Democrats had been battling it out the length and breadth of the state, the Republicans and their nominee, Howard "Bo" Callaway, had been able to relax in the comforting knowledge that the major political polls saw victory for them in the November general election regardless of who emerged victorious among the opposition. These small polls indicated that Callaway's win would not be as simple should Ellis

Arnall be his opponent rather than one of the remaining five. This led to considerable speculation that a crossover Republican vote took place in the Democratic primary, aimed at defeating Arnall. Although this was technically possible, as there was no Republican primary—Callaway having been nominated by petition—and voter registration was not by party, it could not be proved. In my opinion, the allegation was simply being used by opponents of Lester Maddox in an attempt to explain away the 70,000-vote trouncing taken by Arnall in the primary.

The results of the primary were clear-cut in their implication, and I thought it was very well expressed in the heartening response from Alabama's Governor George Wallace:

> It is apparent from Lester Maddox's victory that the people of Georgia want to return to those bedrock principles of our Constitution which guarantee us individual liberty and freedom, the free enterprise system and private property rights. I think we are reaching the turning point in our struggle against federal tyranny and we are well on our way to destroying it. I hope that the people of Georgia and of this nation will continue to make their feelings known in the November elections.

In the case of the Georgia general election, money was to play a very important role. The Republican campaign treasury was bulging. With no primary to finance, with the backing of almost the entire financial community across the state, as well as plentiful aid from the national party, "Bo" Callaway had, if anything, a surplus.

The Democratic coffers were not only empty, they were badly overdrawn. None of this money had been spent in my behalf, rather it had been drained in backing candidates who had opposed me. The deficit, as I went into the campaign as the Democratic candidate, stood at more than $200,000. My own campaign had put me into debt.

I discovered soon enough that large sums of money *are* available to the nominee, but I also knew full well that while these were called "contributions," they were in reality nothing more than advance payments for future favors and preferential treatment, and it was my aversion to this sort of thing that was a factor in my getting into politics in the first place.

I increased the loans against my home and my life insurance to keep the campaign moving along until other legitimate funds could be raised.

In every campaign I have been in, I have received strong support from Republicans, as well as Independents, and this race was no exception. However, the hate-Maddox campaign conducted so long and so relentlessly by much of the media—and especially the Cox newspaper monopoly in Atlanta—had brainwashed many Democrats into the false belief that my nomination would do irreparable damage to the party and my election as governor would set Georgia back to something resembling the Stone Age. These well-intentioned but misguided souls, in seeking to escape their imagined dilemma, organized themselves into "Democrats for Callaway," and became temporary Republicans.

When prominent individuals announced they were "Democrats for Callaway," it made headlines, yet when Democrats announced their support of my candidacy, it never reached the headlines.

Another group, comprised for the most part of liberals of varying degrees, could not align themselves with Maddox or Callaway, and early in October they banded together to launch a write-in campaign. Several prospective candidates reportedly declined the honor and the group finally settled on Ellis Arnall, fresh from his defeat in the primary. Arnall did not overtly accept this "nomination" and he never took an active role in the campaign (known as Write In Georgia, or WIG) but, to my surprise, neither did he repudiate it. I felt that he would surely do this as he had recently indicated during the primary campaign that he was a Democrat with a capital *D*, which I took to mean that if he could not support the candidate of the party, he would certainly not oppose him overtly or covertly.

Callaway immediately complained that WIG was eroding his chances. The truth of the matter was the opposite. WIG was comprised principally of Democrats, people who had supported the liberal Arnall in the primary. Without the write-in campaign, many of them may not have voted at all, the choice being between a conservative Democrat and a conservative Republican. Few, if any, would have swung to Callaway. The majority, being Democrats would have voted Democratic. WIG was, in fact, hurting Lester Maddox far more than it was hurting Callaway.

My own style of campaigning remained the same: as many speeches as I could make and as many hands as I could shake every day. The Callaway forces saturated the state with every imaginable aid—newspaper ads, TV and radio spots, billboards, regional issues of national magazines, and one of the largest and best-paid campaign staffs ever seen in Georgia.

The first time I ran across "Bo" Callaway on the campaign trail was at the Peanut Festival in Sylvester. There was a big parade down the main street of the town with marching bands and Callaway and myself—well separated—riding in open cars. At one corner I got out of the car as I often did to wade into the onlookers and chat and shake hands. I motioned for my driver to move on with the parade and a short time later, when Callaway's car drove into view, I made my way to it and poked out my hand.

"Good to see you, Mr. Callaway!" I said. "I was beginning to wonder if you were still in the race!"

He grinned and climbed out, taking my hand. Newsmen clustered around, cameras flashing. We both got plenty of news coverage that day, but I wondered if my opponent might not have gotten so much if I had not done what I did.

The necessities of running many a money-hungry campaign had taught me to make myself accessible at all times to the press and to try to provide them with something newsworthy and fresh, or at least amusing. I never resorted to canned speeches and if I made a dozen speeches a day I tossed something different into each one so that the newsmen assigned to my campaign would keep their ears open and their pencils and cameras ready. Callaway's tightly organized, almost impersonal organization never achieved the same spontaneity.

The people had put me where I was, not the kingmakers within the political structure as was so often the case, and even though I was the party nominee there were many politicians in the party who were non-plussed as to what to do about Lester Maddox. Some turned their backs, pleading some excuse to be out of the state or even out of the country in order to avoid having to take a stand. One, Representative Charles Weltner of Georgia's Fifth Congressional District, dropped out of his race for re-election rather than support the party's gubernatorial candidate. At least, this was the excuse given. Many knowledgeable observers felt that he made this melodramatic move simply as a way out of certain defeat.

These men fell generally into two groups. First, there were those who feared the unknown. The misinterpretation of my stand at the Pickrick had given them a false image to start with. Here was a man who had never been sanctioned by the Democratic Party in any previous election, a man who had never held public office at any level of government, and suddenly, from out of nowhere as it were, he was nominal head of the party and *their* candidate for the state's top office. This obviously presented a dilemma that many could not cope with and in addition to the splintering caused by WIG, the Democratic ranks were decimated further, by Democrats for Callaway.

Secondly, there were those who had always controlled the nomination. Here came an outsider, Lester Maddox, a man they neither knew nor controlled. These men were the kingmakers, and they were at a loss as to what to do. A new day in the political structure was dawning, and they were helpless to stop it.

I was confident of victory, but as election day drew near, the opinion polls indicated the vote would be close, which cast a more important light on WIG, which might possibly cause neither Callaway nor Maddox to receive the required majority, and while the write-in campaign was not exactly gathering steam it would certainly not die out entirely unless the candidate himself repudiated it.

Callaway continued to complain that he would suffer from the efforts of WIG. Pro-Callaway newspapers (which included virtually every daily in the state) were writing such things as:

A vote for Maddox is a vote for chaos and violence;
A vote for Arnall is a vote for Maddox;
A vote for Callaway is a vote for a bright future for Georgia.

I could not understand the tortured logic that led them to con-
clude that the votes of Democrats siphoned into the write-in campaign would otherwise have gone to a Republican, but I did appreciate the effort they inadvertently gave me in trying to squelch
WIG.

Rumors persisted that Arnall would disavow the whole thing,
but as the days stretched into weeks the likelihood of this lessened.
I made a final effort myself by telephoning him at his home in
Newnan. His response remained exactly as it had been from the
start of WIG.

"I will neither be a party to encouraging a write-in campaign,"
he said, "nor will I be a party to preventing one. It is a completely
free decision for every Georgia voter to make."

That removed any doubt that may have lingered in my mind as
to what Ellis Arnall would do; he would do nothing, and WIG
would continue.

On November 8, 1966, the citizens of Georgia went to the polls.
By 7 P.M., when the polls closed, my headquarters in the Dixie
Ballroom of the Henry Grady Hotel were jammed with people.
Virginia and I arrived an hour later to a tumultuous greeting. Red,
white, and blue bunting decorated the walls of the large room, and
a huge cake, adorned with the great seal of Georgia and a picture
of Lester Maddox, occupied a table to one side, along with bowls
of fruit punch. Everyone was ready for the victory celebration as
the results began to trickle in. The early returns coming in from
the less densely populated rural areas gave me a good margin, and
when less than 5 per cent of the vote had been tallied the three
major television networks were calling me the victor. I was not
convinced and I tried to delay the enthusiasm that swept through
the ballroom. A band was blaring, people were shouting and sing-
ing as if it was all over.

My early lead began to narrow, however, as the returns continued to come in. Midnight rolled around. The early enthusiasts
had worn themselves out. At one o'clock my lead of a few
thousand votes was still inconclusive and I told those remaining
that we should all go home and get some sleep.

While Virginia made coffee the next morning I phoned
headquarters at the hotel.

"The big De Kalb County vote's come in," I was told. "As expected, it went big for Callaway. He's thirty-two thousand ahead."

"We'll be there after breakfast," I said, still not discouraged. "We'll make it up."

It seesawed back and forth throughout the morning and in the afternoon I had edged ahead by a slim margin. It was becoming increasingly apparent that the third factor, WIG, might very well prevent either of us from getting a majority. When all but a trickle of votes were in late on the afternoon of the ninth, both Callaway and Maddox were pushing 450,000 in a virtual tie, and WIG accounted for 50,000. As we looked at the figures my campaign aide, Tommy Irvin, shook his head. "It's going to the General Assembly, Lester."

With no candidate commanding a majority of the vote, the Georgia Constitution requires that the General Assembly, in joint session, shall choose between the two who received the most votes. Not unexpectedly several suits were filed. One, filed in federal court by the American Civil Liberties Union, argued that the U. S. Constitution as well as a number of one-man one-vote Supreme Court decisions would be violated if the state legislature were allowed to elect the governor.

Another suit challenged the legality of the legislature's right to choose the governor, but called for a runoff between Callaway and Maddox, with no write-in vote allowed.

The three-judge Federal Circuit Court quickly found in favor of the plaintiffs, declaring the Georgia Constitution to be invalid in that point. Time was allowed for appeal by the state to the Supreme Court, and in the month that followed there was much speculation on what might happen. There were several possibilities: a rerun of the general election, a runoff strictly between Maddox and Callaway, or, if allowed to go to the legislature, some were even speculating that enough legislators might abstain from voting so that no clear majority would be gained there, and this unlikely event would leave Carl Sanders in the governor's chair. This last possibility went a step further, in that Sanders could swear in Lieutenant Governor-elect George T. Smith, then step down, allowing Smith to become governor.

Of the more likely prospects—a runoff between Callaway and

myself, or the prescribed constitutional process—I felt I would be the winner. If it were the former, I would find myself in the unprecedented position of having to launch my *fourth* campaign of the year.

On December 12, in a five-to-four decision, the U. S. Supreme Court reversed the lower court. The majority opinion, written by Justice Hugo Black, stated that "the United States Constitution does not expressly or impliedly dictate the method a state must use to elect its governor." I was at the University of Georgia in Athens attending a legislative forum when I was called to the phone and told of this decision. The news spread like wildfire through the several hundred legislators and staffers in attendance. It put a sudden end to fence straddling; many who had been cool and non-responsive toward me, were now very visible in the flood of support that swept me up.

As for the decision itself, after having seen the unending meddling of the high court over so many years, during which time it so grossly curtailed individual and states' rights, it was like a breath of unexpected fresh air to see it support the rights of the state of Georgia.

This did not mean the legislature could not itself decline to choose the governor, thus putting the matter back into the hands of the people. Two days after Christmas, another suit was filed, this time in Fulton County Superior Court, to require the legislature to do just that. Judge Claude D. Shaw, however, denied the petition and his action was upheld by the Georgia Supreme Court on January 6.

The legislature was scheduled to go into its regular annual session on January 10, with the first order of business the official canvassing of the general election vote. This, of course, was a legal formality to make the vote official, and the next order of business was the election of the governor.

The legislature was predominantly Democratic, which, in theory at least, gave me the edge. But the legislators themselves were faced with a unique problem, for while I was a Democrat, I was not known to most of them as a political entity. I had not even met most of them, and the ones I did know, I had met in the short time since becoming the standard-bearer after the primary.

With the closeness of the vote between Callaway and myself,

they also had to answer to their own constituents based on the way their constituency went in the general election. The situation was such that a great many of the legislators would have been more than happy to wash their hands of the responsibility entirely. But the last possibility of this disappeared when Legislative Counsel Frank Edwards advised their authority was clear in the state constitution, and that they would have to go ahead with it.

The unusual situation had attracted attention from across the nation, and the three major networks sent crews to cover the session.

The legislature convened on January 9, and the following morning, at nine-thirty sharp, Lieutenant Governor Peter Zack Geer rapped his gavel for order and called the House and Senate into joint session. Television lights blazed in the somber House chamber. The galleries were packed, many of the spectators having waited in line for hours to be assured of a seat.

The canvassing of the vote was to be a long affair, taking the better part of the day. In past elections this had been little more than a formality, but this was no ordinary election and the letter of the law would be followed so that there could be no question of its legality. It was time to get the business of the state moving, and any further delay over who was to be governor the next four years would have been chaotically disruptive.

I remained at the hotel throughout the morning, watching the slow proceedings on television as the sealed returns of Georgia's 159 counties were opened, the results tabulated, and then announced by the lieutenant governor or House Speaker George L. Smith. The counting of the write-in vote was particularly time-consuming due to the numerous ways Ellis Arnall's name was misspelled.

About three that afternoon Virginia and I had a light lunch in the hotel's coffee shop and then drove to the Capitol. In the office of the state auditor we watched the final vote count on a portable television and Lieutenant Governor Geer's announcement of the official tally: 453,665 for Callaway, 450,626 for Maddox, and 52,831 write-ins. It was now official: the Georgia General Assembly would pick the governor, a function that I felt then, and now, would not have been necessary had it not been for WIG. Lester Maddox would have been governor-elect in November.

This process was also presided over by Lieutenant Governor Geer, the man to whom I had lost the runoff four years ago. The inattentiveness and general apathy of the long-drawn-out canvassing were suddenly gone as Mr. Geer began the roll call of senators and representatives. One hundred thirty votes would be needed for election, a majority of the 259-man body. The act of voting turned out not to be a simple response on the part of many of the lawmakers. With their constituents at home watching their every action, some felt constrained to explain their votes, and eleven abstained altogether from voting, even though the lieutenant governor had declared this would not be allowed. Mr. Geer, it should be mentioned, did an outstanding parliamentary job. In fact, had the voters seen his masterful performance before the primary, he probably would have won his own bid for re-election.

I led from the start, quickly widening the gap, and by the time the name of Representative Tom Murphy of Bremen was called— the man I had already asked to be my House leader should I win —he cast the 130th and deciding vote for Maddox.

I jumped up and hugged Virginia. "I knew it!" I said. "I knew it all along!"

As soon as the final vote was cast, giving me 182 to Callaway's 66, I went directly to the executive offices in order to be sworn in as quickly as possible. During the long day it had been rumored that papers would be served on me to prevent my taking office and I wanted the swearing-in done immediately to forestall that possibility, however remote. Surrounded by state troopers, well-wishers, and many old and new political friends, I strode quickly up the broad steps into the rotunda and into the office. Governor Carl Sanders met me there and we shook hands. He asked me how I would like the ceremony handled and I replied that I felt the circumstances called for it being held in private, that it would be repeated the following day publicly in the inaugural ceremony.

Judge Harold Ward, there to perform the swearing-in, asked for a Bible, which was quickly brought.

"Does anyone have a copy of the oath?" the judge asked.

There was a moment of confusion as several people went scurrying about in search of a copy. Minutes later, with a Bible and a copy of the oath, Judge Ward swore me in as the seventy-fifth governor of Georgia. It was 7:30 P.M., January 10, 1967. It was a moment that I never doubted would come, despite the tremendous odds against it.

Some time later, when I was asked how it had happened, I replied, "It really wasn't very difficult. All that was necessary was to defeat the Democrats, the Republicans—on the state and national levels—159 county courthouses, several hundred city halls, the major banks, the railroads, the utility companies, major industry, and all the daily newspapers and television stations in Georgia."

Chapter 8

Starting at the Top

January 11, 1967, was a day a lot of people thought they would
never see. It was Inauguration Day and Lester Maddox was the
man who would stand on the inaugural platform and take the oath
as governor of Georgia. As for myself, I had never lost the
confidence of knowing I would be there, that the cause I stood for
would see to that. During the long months of campaigning, I
would drive back into Atlanta sometimes at three or four o'clock
in the morning and see the gold dome of the Capitol illuminated
against the skyline of the city; I would smile and say to myself, *It
won't be long now*.

I recalled a day back in the summer in the stifling flatland
piney-woods heat of South Georgia when I overheard a man say to
his companion as I made my way through the crowd: "It'll be a
cold day when that fellow gets to be governor of Georgia!"

Sitting there on the platform on the Capitol steps, with the
January wind whipping about us, I could not suppress a smile at
the recollection of that remark. It *was* a cold day even with the
sunshine, thirty-two degrees and dropping, as I recall. We almost
froze before it was over, while in many places around Georgia a
number of politicians were unseasonably warm.

There I was, probably the freest man in the purely political
sense who ever stood there with his hand on the Bible. I looked
out at the thousands of people who had braved the January chill,
old people, young people, people in work clothes, hard-hat steel
workers perched high in the superstructure of a building across the
street. Their victory had put me there.

Beneath the bare trees on the Capitol lawn the cannon fired the traditional salute, aimed merely by chance across Washington Street toward Atlanta City Hall and the offices of my old political foe, Mayor Ivan Allen. The oath was administered and I stood at the podium, my gaze going from face to face. In my address I outlined the plans and programs on which I had campaigned, and then I said: "Law and order will be upheld in Georgia during the Maddox administration. The first responsibility of government is protecting the lives and property of all its people. That responsibility will be met.

"No person need counsel others to engage in riots and disturbances because there will be no need for any person or group to take grievances or problems to the street. . . .

"There will be no place in Georgia during the next four years for those who advocate extremism or violence."

The media seized upon this as though a "new" Lester Maddox had appeared. Headlines, not just in Georgia, but all over the country, stressed one thing: *Maddox Won't Tolerate Extremism or Violence.* It was as though they could not believe what they had heard. So ingrained was my image as a racist, a demagogue, a rabble-rouser, and a mob leader, that it was unthinkable that anyone but a "new" Maddox could have uttered such a statement of moderation and harmony.

Where was the man they thought they knew? Where was the "old" Lester? He had never existed, not as they had painted him. The speech came as no surprise to those who knew me. A man cannot have the true faith in God that I have, and at the same time be the monster I had been made out to be. My inaugural speech was nothing more than a summation of what I believed in, and had always believed in.

I could not be a great surgeon, or a fine artist, or a talented musician, but I *could* be an honest man. I wanted to see what one free and honest man could do as governor of Georgia, one man free from the pressure groups, from all the influences of special interests and political machines.

I ignored the prophets of doom, the ones who said that Lester Maddox would bring ruin on the South's most progressive state. There were others who were concerned because I had never held any elective office, or, for that matter, any position at all in government at any level. They either overlooked the fact, or were unaware, that I had made a study of government for many years. Many were too hasty to listen to the continual references of my being a "high school dropout," without attempting to learn *why* I had been forced to leave school in the tenth grade, or refusing to believe that a man can continue his education himself, as I had done through the years.

Granted, I did not have an intimate knowledge of the inner workings of the government of Georgia based on personal experience. I would have a staff to assist me in this regard. What I did have was a businessman's sense of efficiency and economy. A man who lacks the ability to administer cannot last long in the competition of the private enterprise system—or what is left of that system after the endless inroads of governmental interference. A hardnosed businessman can be a successful administrator in government; the reverse is not necessarily true.

I went into the governor's office on my first working day with the approach of a businessman. It was a going concern; I did not want the momentum interrupted. I knew that the changes of direction that would represent the difference between my administration and the one preceding it would have to be gradual.

With no political debts to pay, there was no problem with political patronage. I kept many of Governor Sanders' staffers because they knew their jobs. To fill the executive offices with all new faces and start from scratch would have been a mistake of the worst kind. As for my Senate and House floor leaders, I had a selling job to do. Of course, I had done this prior to the election in the legislature, but it had not been an easy job to convince the men I wanted. As a body, the legislature was understandably leery of Lester Maddox. I was not a politician in the sense that most of them were. I had not come up through the "ranks," I had done no internship as a county, city, or state official. I was, in a real sense, an unknown factor to them and for an individual to become known as a "Maddox man," before anyone knew who Lester Maddox really was or what he would do, was obviously a politically risky move.

The governor has to have strong floor leaders, men respected by their peers. In order to represent the governor's point of view, they should be men of basically the same political philosophy as the governor.

Representative Tommy Irvin, who had served almost ten years in the House and who had come to me as a campaign aide after I beat Arnall in the Democratic runoff in September, was invaluable in this respect. He knew every member of both houses. Like many of them, he had inevitably made some political enemies along the way, but if there was a man in either the Senate or the House who did not respect Tommy Irvin for his integrity and for standing up for his beliefs, I did not know of him.

"You need someone with political 'savvy,' Lester," he had said to me. In the weeks following the general election in November I had given consideration to numerous possibilities, and had finally settled on the men I wanted. I knew they would be facing bigger obstacles than men holding those positions under previous governors, as it would be inevitable that some of the image of Lester Maddox, created by the biased media, would rub off on them. Taking the job would be the first test of courage.

For one of the toughest and most sensitive jobs, that of executive secretary, I chose a young man whom I first met when he asked me to speak to a group in Athens, Georgia, during my first race for mayor of Atlanta. Young, personable, an Ivy Leaguer, Morgan "Bucky" Redwine and I had become friends over the ten years since that time. This was a job that could more accurately be called "assistant governor," and it required a man who could stand up to the most seasoned and crusty politician and say "no" and make him like it.

For my floor leader in the Senate, I went to another young man, Frank Coggin. Senator Coggin was a former mayor of Hapeville, a municipality in the metro Atlanta area, and just as most politicians, he had opposed me in the past, most notably in his support of Peter Zack Geer in the 1962 lieutenant governor's race. Actually, I had another man in mind for this post, but at the strong suggestion of Lieutenant Governor-elect George T. Smith, I did not name him. I felt that it would not be in the best interest of good government to create an abrasive situation with the presiding officer of the Senate at the very outset.

I made a telephone call to Senator Coggin in late December. "I'd consider it an honor, Senator," I said, "if you would take on the job of floor leader if I'm elected."

He made no effort to conceal his surprise, and I have no doubt he was weighing the consequences of taking on the label of a "Maddox man."

I explained my ground rules. "If you take the job, you, number one, must support my administration. If we differ on occasion, we can work it out in my office. I promise you I'll never embarrass you, and I wouldn't want you to embarrass me."

We worked out an agreement between us and he accepted the job.

I asked Tom Murphy, a veteran legislator from Haralson County, to act as my floor leader in the House. He must have felt the same doubts about the political expediency of the move—that would be only natural—but he accepted.

As Chief of Staff I selected T. Malone Sharpe, a brilliant young lawyer from south Georgia who had been a customer at the Pickrick. This appointment was proof that I held no political grudges, as he had been a supporter of Howard Callaway early in the campaign. Malone Sharpe, who died prematurely some years later, served his state and his profession well, and was a great asset to the Maddox administration.

Another old and trusted friend, Jack Gunter, accepted the job of legal aide, and Bob Short, who had joined in my support in the latter stages of the campaign, became my press secretary.

While some of these appointments were destined to be short-lived, I strove to get what I considered the best possible men for the tasks at hand. I fully understood the initial reluctance of some of them, especially those who were career politicians. Politics is a calling that requires careful deliberation, as past mistakes tend to linger for inordinately long periods of time.

It was a time for fence mending. Georgia had gone through a wrenching time of turmoil created by a steady diet of politics and elections, and more politics and more elections. Through the long months I had been so thoroughly vilified by the racial-liberal segments of the news media that a great many people were simply holding their breath and waiting to see what would happen. It would have been simple to take the easy way out and resort to political expediency. A number of people who had supported me came to me very matter-of-factly expecting a reward, even though I had repeatedly said that would not be my way of operating as governor.

There were occasions when I seemed to baffle both my friends and my foes, an outstanding example being my choice for one of the most important and sensitive posts in the state government, that of revenue commissioner. I have to have a man above reproach from virtually any quarter, and I had a man in mind. I talked to Tommy Irvin about my choice. He registered surprise, but he could only say:

"I don't think you could do any better, if you can get him."

"I think I can get him," I replied confidently.

"You haven't forgotten that he ran against you in '62 for lieutenant governor. And politically, he's liberal."

I had to laugh. "Tommy, there aren't many people I haven't run against during the past ten years!"

The man was Peyton Hawes, a former state senator, an attorney, businessman, and one of the most highly respected figures in Georgia politics.

I phoned him at his office. "Senator," I said, "this is Lester Maddox. I've got something to say to you that may come as a surprise. If you're not sitting down, maybe you should."

"A surprise, Governor? What sort of surprise?"

"I want you to be my revenue commissioner."

There was a moment of silence. "I'm sitting down now," he said. "Would you mind repeating that?"

We talked for quite some time. I told him my feelings about the way appointive posts should be filled, that I was firmly against patronage and firmly for getting the best-qualified people.

"Governor," he said, "I am genuinely honored and flattered that you would call on me as you have. My own feeling is that I should accept. But you were exactly correct in what you said at the outset. You *did* have a surprise for me. In fact, I cannot think of anything that might have come as more of a surprise. I'm honored and faltered that you would call on me for this important position. I believe I'd like to accept, but it comes as such a surprise that I'd appreciate some time in which to consider."

"Of course, Senator Hawes," I said. "Come to see me when you've made your decision."

As soon as it became generally known that Peyton Hawes was considering my proposal, a clamor was heard from both sides. Many people, including at least one of the top men in the Atlanta news media, strongly urged Peyton Hawes to reject the offer, remarking, "Don't go with Maddox! His house will fall!"

His response to this (which he later told me) was to say, "If there is a chance of what you say, and if my serving as a pillar would help prevent it, then I would be shirking my duty as a citizen not to accept!"

A number of those who had supported me complained bitterly on the grounds that Peyton Hawes had not been among their number. He did accept the post, and once the deed was done, even my long and constant adversaries, the Atlanta Cox newspapers, admitted Ol' Lester was doing all right by his appointments.

At the time of my election by the legislature there were eleven Negroes in that body, only one of whom voted for Lester Maddox. Even though Lieutenant Governor Geer, presiding over the session, ruled that no one could abstain from voting one way or the other, ten of these men did abstain.

Shortly after I took office, several of these legislators, along with a number of black business and religious leaders, came to see me at my office in the Capitol. The hour that was to follow was, in my opinion, one of the most significant and important meetings that was to take place in the next four years.

As they entered the room I got up from my desk and walked around to greet them. "How many in your group?" I asked.

One of the spokesmen, State Senator Leroy Johnson, said, "Twenty-five, Governor."

"Seems to me like there're more." I started to count. There were twenty-seven in the delegation and I turned back to Senator Johnson and jokingly said, "If I'd known there were this many of you, I think I would have slipped out the back door!"

There was a ripple of polite laughter as I began to shake hands all around.

Senator Johnson wasted no time in getting to the point of the visit. "Governor Maddox, we have come to tell you that we expect you to issue a directive stating exactly what you're going to do for our people to make up for what men occupying this office previously have failed to do."

"Senator," I interrupted, "if you are here to get me to issue a special directive for *any* special group, then you're at the wrong governor's office! I'm not going to make any special directives for blacks or whites, old or young, Democrats or Republicans, or for any other particular group. The decisions I make as governor are going to be what I consider to be in the best interest of all the citizens of Georgia."

Reverend Martin Luther King, Sr., spoke up firmly: "Governor, you're asking us to wait. We're tired of waiting."

"Preacher," I said, turning and pointing across the broad surface of my desk, "do you see that chair there? I waited on that for more than ten years. I know your people have waited a long time. That doesn't mean we can stop waiting. I intend to work with you and every other citizen of this state, and I intend to see to it that government under my administration is representative and fair and just to everybody."

There was a clamor and several of the delegates tried to speak at once. But I continued.

"By the way, didn't you do everything in your power to elect the governor who preceded me?"

Several heads nodded. "Yes."

"What sort of an effort did you make to put me in this office?"

"We worked as hard as we could to get Governor Sanders elected, but we fought even harder to beat you."

I smiled. "Well, don't feel like the Lone Ranger! I beat more whites than I beat blacks. Regardless of your opposition in the past, with your understanding and help and co-operation, I'm going to try to be the best governor this state ever had, and I can't possibly do that by working against any group of citizens or creating any special conditions for any other group. So, even though you have fought for some of my predecessors and by your own words, fought even harder to keep me out, I want to assure you I'll do as much for you as my predecessor did."

"Lord!" someone piped up. "Governor, *please* do more than that!"

That brought a laugh from everyone.

"Well," I said, "I will if you don't fight me. But if you just want to fight Lester Maddox, then what happened at the Pickrick will be nothing compared to what will happen if I'm fought as governor. As the leaders of your community I want your help in keeping order and upholding the peace. If I get that help from you, then I *can* and *will* do more for you than any other governor has ever done."

The meeting went on for more than an hour. I think the "image" of Lester Maddox may have caused them to listen as they did. Here was their arch enemy—at least, they had been led to believe this— offering them all he could. My sincerity in what I said must have come through, and they seemed to sense that everything they had read and heard about Lester Maddox was not necessarily true, and that I was, in fact, free from the political constraints that had bound the men occupying this office before me. I was free to attempt the lofty goals I had set, and they knew it.

When the delegation left my office, if they did not go with a total expression of confidence, at least it was much closer to that than it was to the mood in which they had arrived. I have no doubt that it had a tremendous impact on the four years that lay ahead.

This meeting bore fruit on more than one occasion, perhaps the most graphic being some time later during the picketing of a major shoe store in downtown Atlanta. The situation was becoming extremely tense, with black pickets lying on the floor, trying on dozens of shoes, and putting a halt to the conduct of business. The mayor of the city was unable or unwilling to take effective action in any form, and I called some of these same black leaders.

"For goodness sake!" I said. "Stop this! If this thing blows up— and it looks as if it will—you're putting a roadblock in my path. We need reason and compromise if you're going to leave me free to do what I said I would!"

We talked at length and they agreed to give it a chance. The pressure was removed, and the problem worked out between the black community and store owners in a peaceful fashion.

Virginia and the children and I moved into the old governor's mansion in Ansley Park, a fine old Atlanta neighborhood. A new mansion was under construction on the north side of the city, but its completion was many months off. I had been to the mansion before moving there—three times as a caterer and one time at a reception. During the administration of Governor Marvin Griffin, the Pickrick had been low bidder on three occasions to cater various affairs. On one of these I had bid so closely that Governor Griffin's fifty-dollar tip, when it was all over, represented the

Pickrick's profit. The farthest thing removed from my imagination at that time was that I would ever be the occupant of that house.

In the beginning, Virginia and the children saw a lot more of the mansion than I did. In the normal course of events the governor-elect of Georgia in the past had from September to January to prepare himself and his program for the first session of the legislature. Until the 1966 elections, there had been no Republican opposition of consequence, and the Democratic primary had been tantamount to election. Even in this election with two-party representation, the governor-elect might have been assured of a two-month period for this preparation. In my case I had absolutely no time. I went from Democratic nominee to governor in the time it took to walk from one office in the Capitol to another, with a few minutes to spare while someone tried to find a copy of the oath of office. I thanked God that my long study of government and my long experience in business enabled me to step into this high office without fear or trepidation.

The state was fortunate under these unusual circumstances to have a man of Governor Carl Sanders' caliber in office at the time. Following the indecisive November election, Governor Sanders had invited Mr. Callaway and me to go through the intricate process with him and his staff as they prepared a budget proposal for presentation to the legislature. This statesmanlike approach to the problem was of tremendous help to me when I took office. A man of less stature might easily have turned his back on the situation, which would not only have compounded the difficulties facing the incoming governor, but would have had a generally disruptive effect on the governmental processes and, in the end, the people of Georgia.

Even so, the job commanded my entire attention in the early weeks. I spent seven days and seven nights a week at it; it was my business and my hobby, my golf, my fishing, my partying. I had worked hard all my life, but I can say with complete candor that the first weeks in which I occupied the office of governor were the toughest I had ever gone through. And, perhaps, the most satisfying.

Chapter 9

Some Changes in the Old Ways

If there was a key plank in my platform during the campaign, it was honesty and efficiency in government. That was at the heart of all four of the races I had made. Of these, honesty is the uppermost. There can be no doubt that lack of honesty in government will cloud all other aspects of it; Watergate and similar instances at other levels of government refute any argument to the contrary.

In my three losing races, and up until the attempt during the 1966 primary to buy me out of the race, I had not personally experienced the temptations that come the way of many candidates and officeholders. This quickly changed almost as soon as my victory over Ellis Arnall had been confirmed. Support flocked to my side, not unexpectedly, but among those who came were some who were not aware that the old ways had changed. Big cars and men in expensive suits were in evidence where they had not been before and, as it developed, some of them were motivated by less than lofty ideals.

My brother Wesley had temporarily closed down his contracting business to help me during the campaign, and on several occasions he was approached as a sort of "go-between" for offers of money. He came to me in my small office at campaign headquarters one morning.

"Lester, there's a fellow out there who says he can get up $150,000 for the campaign if you'll just sit down with this friend of his and have a talk with him."

I leaned back in my chair and shook my head. "Now, why do

you suppose a man would offer that kind of money to talk to me when all he's got to do is knock on the door and he can talk free?"

Wesley chuckled. "It is kind of peculiar, isn't it?"

"Tell him we can't use his $150,000, but I'll be glad to talk to him any time."

That was only the start of it. If I had taken even a small portion of the "campaign contributions" that were literally pushed at me, I could have had my picture on just about every billboard in Georgia, with enough left over to pre-empt all the reruns of "I Love Lucy" and "Leave It to Beaver."

It did begin to worry Wesley. He told me of this concern one day as we walked to an appointment in downtown Atlanta.

"I never saw anything like it, Lester. You'd think some of these people have got money growing on trees. You know, it's sort of like that thing in Macon. If they want to give you all this money and you don't take it, maybe they'll use it somewhere else, like *against* you."

We walked into the lobby and paused at the elevators. "We can't help that, Wesley. The big money people want to buy something— or somebody—and they can't buy me. I'm not for sale."

The elevators doors opened and we got in and I punched the button for the floor. "Suppose I'm sitting there in the governor's office and a fellow comes in one day and says he wants this or that favor, or wants my help in getting a state contract or something, and he just happens to remind me that he put up $150,000 when *I* needed it. A man would be on the spot. No, sir, Wesley, that kind of money is not a campaign contribution. It's a down payment, and we're not taking one dime of it!"

It was difficult getting some people to understand this, even though I did everything I could to make it abundantly clear. Some seemed to sense it, but had to make the attempt regardless. When one man came to me he said, "I know I shouldn't do this, Lester, but the group I represent wants to put up $100,000 toward your campaign. How about it?"

I told him he already knew the answer or he wouldn't have said he shouldn't do it.

Another fellow came to me with what he must have thought was pretty strong support. He said that the Lord had told him to give me the money.

"Well, since then," I replied, "the Lord told me not to take it!"

Now that I was governor, there would have been far more pigeons coming home to roost at the Capitol than all the statues on the grounds could have accommodated—if I had taken the offers that had been turned down. As it was, a few small birds fluttered in. One man who had contributed to my efforts in all my campaigns (although he obviously misunderstood me) came to me and said he wanted me to get him a job with the state. I told him to apply for whatever job he wanted and if he was qualified and there was an opening he would have as good a chance as anyone else.

He gave me a knowing smile and nodded toward the telephone. "Come on, Lester, all you got to do is pick that thing up and say the word and I've got the job. Look, I've been kicking in to you ever since you ran against Hartsfield."

"How much would you say you've . . . 'kicked in'?"

"I can tell you exactly how much! I kept a record of it! It's six hundred and twenty-one dollars!"

I nodded and reached into my inside coat pocket and took out a checkbook. I wrote out a check for the amount, signed it, and handed it to him. "Now, you and I are even! If you still want that state job, let me suggest that you do what I said. I don't make phone calls about jobs—one way or the other."

I informed all the departments in state government, and I made these statements public, that they were to hire the best-qualified people for whatever job might be open. Applicants were not to be rated as black or white, pro- or anti-Maddox, or in any way other than job qualification. I thought I had made this abundantly clear while I was campaigning, but this gentleman was proof that some people had either not heard it, or did not believe it if they had.

There were changes in the early months of my administration, not only in some of the ways things were done, but in some of my top level appointments. Jack Gunter, my legal aide, resigned to be replaced by Frank Blankenship. An Emory University graduate student, Jack Thomas, joined my staff in the part-time capacity of speech writer, and later replaced Bob Short as my press secretary. My executive secretary, Morgan "Bucky" Redwine, and I had a disagreement and by mutual agreement, Bucky tendered his resignation. The sensitivity of this particular job, being in essence the "assistant governor," called for extreme care in the choice of a successor. My first choice was the young man who had come to me during the campaign, to become a top aide, Tommy Irvin, the representative from Habersham County. He had been of inestimable help to me through his keen political insight, and I felt that if I combed the state I could find no better man for the job. Some of my old friends opposed the choice, apparently feeling that Tommy was *too* political, but my mind was made up and I called him and told him what I wanted.

Of course, the decision was up to him. He had represented his county for many years, and had just been elected to a new two-year term in the House. There were obvious possibilities of political liability in hitching one's wagon to Lester Maddox, and I am sure Tommy Irvin weighed these carefully against the relative security of the position he had. His decision was not slow in coming.

"I appreciate the honor, Governor," he said, "and I accept."

It was not long before many of those who had been opposed to the appointment agreed that Tommy Irvin was the ideal man for the job, and he performed an invaluable service to the early difficult months of my administration.

I have always firmly believed that campaign promises should be carried out to the letter, and one thing I had promised was more direct involvement of the people in their government. One way I attempted this was to set aside the first and third Wednesdays of each month as "People's Day," a time when anyone who wished could come to see me personally to air a complaint, pass along an idea or suggestion, or just shake hands and say hello. The first of these semi-monthly sessions was held scarcely a week after I took office, and from a modest beginning they grew to such proportions that I had brought in representatives of various state departments —Veterans, Health, Corrections, and others—to counsel the people on specific problems and requests.

It was tiring to meet several hundred citizens individually in an afternoon, but I feel it was one of the greatest experiences of my life. Many problems, from the overview of government, tend to boil down into cold statistics. "People's Day" reversed that tendency, and I saw more sorrow, frustration, and sadness than should exist, and I had the incomparable satisfaction in many cases of being in a position to alleviate it. I believe this not only made a better public official of me and the others who worked in this unusual program, but better human beings as well.

As I stood in my office one Wednesday, the line stretching ahead of me and into the corridor, I shook hands with each individual and listened to problems concerning a loved one in prison, or in the state hospital, or some problem of taxes, and when each problem had been defined I would turn the person over to an appropriate aide.

After talking to a hundred or more citizens I reached for the next hand in line. The man was of medium height, neatly though not expensively dressed, with the tanned and weathered face of a dirt farmer.

"Yes, sir," I said. "Good to see you! What can I do for you?"

He gripped my hand firmly. "You can't do a thing for me, Governor. I just wanted to shake your hand!"

I chuckled and turned quickly to an aide, Reverend Cliff Brewton. "Preacher!" I said. "Get a cameraman, quick! I want my picture taken with this gentleman! I asked him what he wanted, and he said he didn't want *anything!*"

This idea, incidentally, proved so successful that the man who succeeded me as governor, Jimmy Carter, committed himself to continue it, even if he did so on a lesser scale.

In addition to these public sessions at the Capitol, the mansion was open to the public from Sunday through Friday, with Virginia acting as hostess. Sometimes on Sunday afternoon I would find time to join her in welcoming our guests. These were generally pleasant, relaxed, informal affairs attended by neighbors, friends, legislators, preachers, and ordinary citizens from all walks of life. In fact, they came from some rather unexpected walks of life at times. One sunny April Sunday an expected crowd of two thousand turned out to be more than twice that number, with long lines of visitors winding down the driveway at the old mansion on Atlanta's Prado. Virginia and I greeted each in turn, chatting, shaking hands, and offering punch and cookies to all.

Four young black men, shabbily dressed and accompanied by an older woman, came through the line. As they moved past me I noticed the woman talking quietly and seriously with Virginia. They moved on, Virginia going with them, and a few moments later one of the state troopers on duty came to me and whispered, "Governor, something unusual has happened. Those four young blacks who just came through the line would like a word in private with you. It seems they broke out of prison in south Georgia last night. We have them under guard in the summer house."

I went with him. The four young men and the mother of one of them were waiting patiently with Virginia and another officer. For the next quarter of an hour I listened to a horror story of abuse, deprivation, inadequate sleeping and sanitary facilities, and instances of unusual punishment as the four told of life in a Georgia prison camp. I did not know whether they were telling the truth or not. They said that they had not escaped only to gain freedom, but for the purpose of coming to me to explain the conditions of their imprisonment in the hope that I would do something about it. Obviously, if freedom had been their aim, they would not voluntarily be where they were at that moment, talking to the governor and in custody of the police. They would probably be headed for California, New York, or anywhere else far from Georgia. The circumstances demanded immediate investigation, and I interrupted briefly and turned to one of the troopers:

"Telephone Bob Carter [assistant head of the Corrections Department] and tell him I would like him to get over here right away."

Subsequent investigation of the particular camp tended to support most—if not all—the charges made by the men. Continuing investigation into the entire prison system revealed that this was not an isolated case. One of the most incredible cases that came to light involved an incident that took place in December 1966, just prior to my election. A prisoner had allegedly volunteered his services to a guard who was shooting ducks over a pond. The prisoner had stripped off his clothes in the dead of winter and dived into the freezing water to retrieve the ducks shot by the guard. The man had drowned in his efforts.

Asked if I believed that a man would volunteer to do a thing like this in thirty-four-degree weather, I stated: "You show me how many people believe this, and I'll show you how many fools we've got in the state of Georgia."

Long overdue reform of the prison system resulted from these

investigations. I proposed legislation that set forth minimum re-
quirements for fire and health standards, clothing, adequate training
for guards and other prison personnel, and many other changes in
state and local penal institutions and camps.

I also envisioned a program which I felt would be of great value.
This was the early release of prisoners, men and women whose
prison terms had only a short time to run and whose records as in-
mates were good. This had been tried in various prison systems
around the country, but only on a small scale. I felt strongly that
early release could be very effective in rehabilitation and in cutting
down on the alarming rate of recidivism in our prison populations,
as well as accomplishing the immediate practicality of relieving overcrowded prisons.

The Georgia Industrial Institute, a prison for youthful offenders
which was located in Alto, was chosen for the experiment. Careful
evaluation was made of nearly 10 per cent of the boys in the institution, some with only a few days or weeks, some with up to six
months still to serve. I had visited Alto myself and seen the
overcrowded conditions, and when some 153 boys had been
chosen they were given new clothes and brought by bus to the
Capitol. The parents and other loved ones of many of the youths
were waiting there for them.

They were assembled in the House chamber, where I spoke to
them. "If you fail to live as law-abiding citizens—and I don't think
you're going to fail—they'll be after your governor. I'm sticking
my neck out for you, way out, and it won't get chopped off if you
don't chop it off. I don't believe one of you is going to fail me. I
want you to prove to your mothers and fathers, to state officials, to
everyone, that you can do it."

I was counting on this action to give the boys a feeling that
someone had confidence in them, enough, in fact, to risk criticism.
After state School Superintendent Jack Nix, Labor Commissioner
Sam Caldwell, and others had a word with the youths, they signed
a pledge that they would "go straight," and then they were allowed
to go on their ways.

Criticism of the early release of so many young men, and not
minor offenders for the most part, was to be expected. And only
time would prove me or my critics right.

Several months later the records showed that only a few had

gotten into trouble and wound up back in jail. Most were working or going to school. The pilot program was a success. With Christmas approaching, the program was broadened to include not only youthful offenders, but men and women from the state prisons and county work camps. More than five hundred convicts were included in this early release, approximately 7 per cent of the prison population. The releases granted these people, none, of course, of whom were incorrigibles or in for heinous crimes, were effective December 1 so that they could find jobs before Christmas and have a little money to brighten up the season with their loved ones. I told them the same thing I had told the youngsters that preceded them, and I added, "If this program is successful, we'll probably do it again. Don't penalize those who are to follow. And just a final word. Other ways have failed. Try turning to Him Whose birthday we shall soon celebrate, Whose Spirit is responsible for your being free and Who said, 'I am the way . . .' Try it. It worked for me. I wouldn't 'con' you. Good luck!"

And 547 ex-convicts walked out of the Capitol as free people. By the following August only thirteen of these people had run afoul of the law, and ten of these were for public drunkenness. With the first two groups having done almost unbelievably well, another ninety-five from the Alto institution were given release in August. The program was a calculated risk and it has been continued on the basis of its success.

Among the many voices crying out in despair as I went into the general election of 1966 as the Democratic standard-bearer was that of a prominent Georgia psychiatrist. He predicted "four years of Federal troops and racial demonstrations if Lester Maddox is elected governor," and suggested that my election might also drive away billions of dollars in tourist business because "tourists will be afraid to come into or through Georgia." He went on to say that my election would "give Stokely Carmichael, the SNCC firebrand, a governor he will fight with and demonstrate against for four desperate years. Do you want Federal troops in our state during the next four years? Do you want industry to look at Georgia with a wary eye and turn away?"

Dr. Corbett Thigpen, co-author of the best seller *The Three Faces of Eve,* made these statements in all sincerity, and he was

19. Virginia and I with our good friends Lurleen and George Wallace. Lurleen was newly elected governor of Alabama when this picture was taken in January 1971.

20. With Atlanta mayor Ivan Allen, Jr.

21. These children were in the athletic program for under-privileged children sponsored by Fort Stewart Army Base.

22. I officially opened the final link of Interstate.285, Atlanta's perimeter highway, June 25, 1970. Chamber of Commerce and Georgia Department of Industry and Trade
officials suggested that we open the highway in this fashion,
and I agreed. (Photo by Joe McTyre)

23. Joining the famous Graham W. Jackson in a few choruses. (Photo by Dwight Ross)

24. Attending Gold Rush Day in Dahlonega, Georgia, in 1973, while I was lieutenant governor.

far from being alone in his concern. Yet, long before my four-year term as governor had been completed Dr. Thigpen had become a staunch supporter of mine.

Why? He was a dedicated man of medicine, not a politician; it could hardly be for political reasons. The simple fact was, his fears proved to be without foundation. No substantial change took place in either Dr. Thigpen or in Lester Maddox. Of course, I knew that the predictions were groundless. Those who really knew me were well aware of this, and those who came to know me—Dr. Thigpen and many, many more who shared his feelings—also came to know this.

The truth was, the very things that had been pointed out as being in jeopardy should I be elected were important goals in my administration. Tourism and the growth of industry were both vital parts of the economic lifeblood of Georgia and at the time I took office the state was in the sad predicament of being close to the bottom of the list in the South in new and expanded industry. There was an agency, the Department of Industry and Trade, whose function was ostensibly to publicize and promote Georgia, and to actively seek out industry and to stimulate tourism. Over this department was a board comprised of twenty men, all leaders in their communities. In practice, however, this board exercised little power over the workings of the department, and down through the years Industry and Trade had, unfortunately, degenerated into little more than a political dumping ground and playhouse. If there were political favors to be repaid, I&T provided a convenient pay-out window.

I had campaigned on the cleanup of this department (among others), and I immediately called for the dismissal of the director, and for the appointment of a new man, someone absolutely independent of political pressure. I met with strong opposition; the political/commerce establishment exerted great pressure behind handpicked candidates for the post. As the months dragged by with Industry and Trade caught in this tug-of-war, my critics wasted no opportunity to say that Lester Maddox was "adrift in a sea of confusion." The truth was that I was not adrift at all, but rowing as hard as I could in an effort to buck the tide of entrenched politics and special interest groups.

This was my first major confrontation, the first serious obstacle to my drive for efficiency in government. Defeat here would have a tremendous impact on my future effectiveness, and those who opposed me were just as aware of this as I was. I had taken this problem before the people during the campaign, and I continued to do so now. The result was that my persistence finally broke the stalemate. The director and the board chairman resigned, clearing the way for the cleanup of the department.

The problem remained of finding the man for the job. A number of names were submitted, and by agreement with the board that I would have the prerogative of okaying any nominee, they were all rejected. Then one day Mr. Courtney Wynne phoned me.

"I hear you're having trouble finding the right man to head up the Department of Industry and Trade," he said.

"It's a tough thing, Courtney, finding an able man who hasn't got some ax to grind."

"I've got a suggestion you might consider," he went on. "I'm sure you know General Louis Truman."

"The commandant of the Third Army at Fort McPherson? Yes, I've met him on several occasions."

"Did you know that he's due for retirement from the Army very soon, and that he is sold on Georgia and plans to make his home here after he retires? He's a highly qualified man, Lester, and a challenge such as this job might appeal to him."

It was an exciting suggestion. General Truman, a cousin of former President Harry Truman, possessed an excellent reputation as an officer and administrator, and while he knew personally a great many influential people in Georgia, he was not a political figure.

I wasted no time in phoning him at Third Army Headquarters. I told him of my conversation with Courtney Wynne. "We both agree that you would be the ideal man for the job, General Truman. Of course, there are a great many things to iron out, such as outlining the duties you would have, the overall program of the department, and not the least important, the board's approval of the appointment."

General Truman confirmed his imminent retirement, and said that he was very pleased to hear from me and would be delighted to consider the proposition, tentative as it was.

I then went to the acting chairman of the board, and told him of my conversation with Louis Truman. Members of the board were contacted, and at the meeting my nomination of General Truman met with unanimous approval. He accepted the offer, and upon retiring from the Army, and after a short period of time to arrange his affairs relating to retirement, as well as a well-earned vacation, General Louis Truman assumed the directorship of the department.

I consider this one of the important accomplishments of my administration. Industry and Trade had been operating on an annual advertising budget of $200,000. I requested, and got, an increase to $500,000. Under the effective direction of General Truman, results were not slow in coming. Where mismanagement and political interference had dribbled away the department's funds in previous years, the entire budget was now directed into dynamic new approaches. Provocative ads were placed in national publications. Georgia became the first state to advertise on national television programs such as the "Today Show," with impressive results.

As chief executive I made numerous industry-seeking trips all over the country, along with General Truman and leaders of business and industry. From my days at the Pickrick I have always believed in the value of personal contact in public relations. Occasionally, if I found myself with spare time in my schedule, I would call on some prospect without an appointment, just to introduce myself. I recall one such visit in Chicago, where I dropped in to an office on the thirty-ninth floor of a downtown building.

I walked up to the receptionist's desk. "Good morning, young lady. My name's Lester Maddox. Would you please tell your boss I'd appreciate a few minutes of his time?"

She went into the inner office and a few moments later the president of the company came out with her. We shook hands and went into his office, observing the usual amenities. As we sat down a scaffold carrying two window washers lowered slowly to the broad windows behind the gentleman's desk. I noticed that the windows were hinged, and I got up, opened one of them, and poked my hand out.

"Good morning, friend! I'm Lester Maddox! Nice to see you!" I shook his hand and then reached to shake hands with his coworker.

I then resumed my conversation with the company president.

Half an hour later, as I walked out of the building onto the sidewalk, I was surprised to see the two window washers standing talking to a group of their fellow workers. I walked over to them.

One of them grabbed my hand. "Here he is! The governor of
Georgia! The man who opened the window on the thirty-ninth
floor to shake hands with us!"

That called for another round of handshaking. You never know;
today's window washer may be tomorrow's company president.

On a visit to Akron, Ohio, General Truman and I, along with
several Goodyear executives from Georgia, called on Goodyear's
board chairman, Mr. Russell DeYoung.

I had hardly had time to say "Hello" when Mr. DeYoung buttonholed me with: "What are you doing about those speed traps
down there in Georgia!"

I replied, half jokingly, "Speed traps? Somebody's spreading
rumors up here!"

"Rumors *hell!*" Mr. DeYoung laughed. "It wasn't any rumor
that one of our executives got picked up last week in Ludowici,
Georgia!"

I was painfully aware of the reputation that that particular town
had gained over the years. I told Mr. DeYoung that I would look
into it as soon as I got home. It was not a simple matter, nor did I
think it would be. Administrations before mine, including that of
my predecessor, Carl Sanders, had taken steps to clean up such
abuses. It was not merely the problem of Ludowici and Long
County, but other localities as well. And, of course, the practice
was by no means exclusive with Georgia.

It was embarrassing, to say the least, to find myself confronted
with this sort of shabby con game while attempting to talk business
with the head of a major manufacturing firm.

The standard practice of the speed trap, as was the case in
Ludowici, was to extend the low speed limit of the town far out
onto the open highway. In the open countryside, few motorists
would observe the unreasonable limit of twenty-five or thirty miles
per hour, and they would quickly find themselves being pulled
over by a local policeman.

The motorist would be required to post a cash bond in order to
continue on his way. The traffic case would be scheduled for some

future date, by which time the motorist would be hundreds of miles away. The bond would be forfeited in view of the complete impracticality of returning to face trial.

I contacted the Long County authorities and warned them that the practice would have to cease. I also appealed to the good people of the county to make an effort to convince their officials of the harm such actions were doing to the good name of their area, not to mention the state as a whole.

It made little sense to spend hundreds of thousands of dollars to promote tourism and to try to attract industry and at the same time allow the greed of a few local officials to endanger those efforts. As was generally the case when pressure was applied, the speed traps cooled down for a time. Slowly, the complaints would begin to trickle in again and the process would be repeated. I kept the pressure on, and was even commended by the American Automobile Association and others for my efforts.

The good citizens of Ludowici and Long County were apparently responding by pressuring their local officials. However, as is invariably the case in these affairs, the officials who engage in these unsavory practices do not possess the vision to see the harm they do. Oddly, they even think *their* rights are being infringed upon. A few months after I began my efforts to stamp out the speed traps, a delegation of local officials, headed by Mr. Ralph Dawson, showed up at my office.

Mr. Dawson assumed an attitude of self-righteousness and arrogance at the outset.

"Governor," he said, "the way you've been fighting us and all the publicity you've been getting is hurting our county, and we want you to stop it!" There was a murmur of approval from the group of about twenty-five.

"Mr. Dawson," I replied, "you can sit there and tell me that I'm hurting your county?"

"There wouldn't be all this in the newspapers if it wasn't for you."

I walked around my desk and stood before him. "You're not just hurting Long County. You're hurting the good people in that county! You're hurting the whole state of Georgia, and still you've got the gall to come here—" I took a step closer to where he was seated and aimed a finger at him. "You're the most corrupt, dishonest, nastiest, and crookedest person ever to come into my office! The longer you stay here, the longer it's going to take to clean it up when you're gone!"

With that I took hold of his arm and, pulling him up from the chair, began to march him unceremoniously toward the door.

He tried to twist loose. "Wait a minute!" he said angrily. "Let me get my hat!"

"I'm going to throw you out first, and your hat next!" I shoved him out into the corridor, walked back and picked up his hat, and sailed it out after him.

I turned back toward the remaining members of the group. "Did each of you gentlemen hear what I had to say to Mr. Dawson?"

They responded in the affirmative. I added: "Then I want you to know that if you feel the way he does, that wrongdoing should be excused and that it's wrong for Lester Maddox to try to clean it up, what I said to Mr. Dawson goes for you too!"

No one else chose to continue the illogical argument Dawson had tried to start. I tried to make it abundantly clear to them that wherever conditions detrimental to the state existed, I would do my level best to get rid of them.

Corrupt officials in several counties continued to allow numerous abuses that gave Georgia a bad name. Crooked operators of gas stations would drain the oil out of a customer's car while he was in the rest room or otherwise occupied, and fleece him for the repairs that would have to be made a short way down the road. There were numerous con games, illegal gambling, illegal whisky at roadside stands along the north and south routes.

A call came into my office one day from the Better Business Bureau in Savannah. A New Hampshire couple had stopped to complain of being fleeced in a nearby county. They were advised to go back to the county seat and file a complaint. They did this— and promptly wound up in jail under $1,000 bond as material witnesses in the case.

I immediately telephoned the sheriff of the county and told him to turn them loose. "If I find out they're still there an hour from now," I told him, "I'm going to fly down there and turn them loose myself!"

The only way a cleanup of these conditions could ever work was to arouse the decent citizens in the communities where it was going on, and I took my case to them, visiting the towns and counties and urging the people to get things straight by ridding themselves of the crooked politicians who allowed such unhealthy practices to flourish. Even so, it took constant efforts on the part of my administration throughout the four years to keep these things under control.

In the case of the speed traps in Ludowici, at one point I had billboards placed on the highways at the county line, warning motorists of the danger that lay head. State patrolmen were kept on sentry duty around the clock to keep the signs from being removed by the speed trap operators. Eventually, the righteous indignation of the good people of Long County corrected the problem at the polls.

We did not expend all our efforts simply to correct bad conditions, but tried in every way possible to make Georgia attractive to visitors. I often stopped in at our official welcome centers located on major highways at the state line and personally greeted travelers.

One day in late autumn Senator Frank Coggin came to my office and informed me that the Hapeville High School band, from his district, had been selected to participate in the Tournament of Roses Parade, preceding the New Year's Day Rose Bowl Game in Pasadena, California.

"I know the state can't contribute to the band's expense fund," he went on, "but I've got an idea that might be worth considering. What about Georgia entering a float in the parade?"

I was immediately struck by the possibilities and Senator Coggin and I discussed it with General Truman. We all agreed it was certainly worth looking into, and the Tournament of Roses officials were contacted. Float builders worked out various designs and brought models of their handiwork to Atlanta. Costs of the floats ranged from about $15,000 to more than $40,000. One immediately caught my fancy, for its simplicity of design and special representation of Georgia. It was an Old South scene, with a columned mansion reminiscent of *Gone With the Wind*'s Tara. And the price tag was only $19,000.

"That's the one," I said to General Truman and the others who were present. "That's it, and I'll predict that it'll take first prize in the competition!"

We agreed on it, signed the contract, and the float builders went back to California to get started. The bill was paid out of the governor's special emergency fund. No sooner did word of this get out than the Atlanta news media jumped on me for squandering the taxpayers' money. I stood by my guns, even though the attack on me continued right up until the start of the parade on New Year's Day.

Shortly after I heard an Atlanta radio station criticizing me I tuned in the parade on television and heard that Georgia's float had indeed won first prize. National television coverage, along with local television stations all over the country showing it on film or tape, plus the story running in newspapers from coast to coast amounted to at least $1.25 million in advertising for an outlay of only $19,000.

All I could say to my critics, who were now noticeable only by their silence, was: "I don't know how to get any more for our money than that!"

Chapter 10

Four Short Years

It was not until late in 1967 that the Maddox family moved into the new multimillion-dollar governor's mansion, and even then it was in an unfinished condition. I had observed what I interpreted as a peculiar slowdown in construction after I became governor, and I considered the possibility that this had something to do with the fact that a different tenant might have been envisioned when the plans were laid. Whether by coincidence or not, the job gathered speed once we were in, and it was soon completed.

There had been considerable controversy over building the mansion in the first place. Many critics had questioned the high cost and where the priority of such an expenditure should fit into the budget. This was one controversy Lester Maddox was not involved in; the mansion had obviously not been designed for us, as there was a bedroom for the governor and another for the governor's wife.

A minor furor did develop over one change I made in the plans. I deleted a swimming pool and added a fence. Here we had what was perhaps the finest executive mansion of any state in the nation, costing well over two million dollars, on a large tract of land, and no fence around it. The original plans called for a security checkpoint at the front door, which meant that anyone who wanted to ring the governor's doorbell at any time of day or night had only to walk up and do so. So I authorized a fence to be built, not only for security but for aesthetic purposes as well. While this was a minor expense compared to the overall cost, it was all that was necessary to bring forth squeals from the Atlanta news media and other Maddox-haters.

As soon as the mansion was completed, Virginia and I held it open to the public every Sunday through Friday. This had very favorable results, not only with the Georgia citizens who paid for it, but with visitors from outside the state as well, and as far as I know it was a "first." While I was never there during the weekdays, and only occasionally on Sundays because of the heavy demands of my office, Virginia graciously carried out the duties of being hostess. The goodwill created in this way was incalculable. Out-of-state visitors expressed surprise at being able to tour the mansion almost any day of the week, and were especially pleased to meet the first lady, and occasionally, the governor, on such an informal, personal note. Apparently some of these people took the story home with them, for Virginia began to get letters from other first ladies asking her advice on how to conduct these daily public affairs, and the practice caught on in varying degrees in some of our sister states.

There was one amusing sidelight to the publicity this generated, and that was columnist Jack Anderson's report that Lester Maddox was neglecting his job as governor of Georgia while electing to stay at home to play with his basset hounds. A report which was, incidentally, fairly representative of Mr. Anderson's usual inaccuracy.

The atmosphere of serenity, gentility, and calm that prevailed in the new mansion, I feel, had repeatedly justified its existence. On at least one occasion it played a part in saving an industry for Georgia. A major manufacturer had announced plans for a new plant in the southern part of the state, and in negotiating for this important industry, the local taxing officials had made some attractive concessions to the company. However, another company, in an unrelated field, let it be known that it objected to this and was planning to file a suit alleging preferential treatment. Efforts to convince his company's officers that the state would lose the new industry entirely should such a suit be filed had gotten nowhere, and as the last day rolled around, I asked the officers of the complaining company to meet me for breakfast at the mansion for a discussion of the problem.

As a result of a leisurely Georgia breakfast, the surroundings so conducive to calm deliberation, and a relaxed talk, the gentlemen agreed to abandon their plans for a lawsuit. The new industry moved ahead with the building of its plant, and in the years since then it has spent more than $100 million in capital investments, not to mention the tax revenue and the tens of millions of dollars in wages that it has generated.

There were, of course, a lot of well-known faces seen around the mansion that were never seen at the Pickrick. One of these callers, during the early months of my administration, while we were still living at the old mansion, was Vice-President Hubert Horatio Humphrey. While we were quite a distance apart in our political philosophies, that in no way diminished the personal charm of Mr. Humphrey, and in that sense it was always a pleasure to see him. This first meeting was seen as being very newsworthy by the media, and when his visit was announced there was a large contingent from the news media on hand to record it for posterity.

Before we went out to meet the press, we talked for quite some time in private. I made a strong effort to impress on him my views on the mistaken direction that had been taken by the national administration. I pointed out how many of their programs, while well intentioned, were penalizing industriousness and attempting to make luxury the reward of slothfulness.

"Mr. Vice-President," I said, "do you believe in private enterprise in this country?"

"Of course I do, Governor!"

"Do you know, I've never heard you use the expression? The programs of the federal government today are working full time toward the destruction of that system. If you really believe in it, go out and tell the people!"

It was not merely a chance visit. The national Democratic Party had fared poorly in the South and Mr. Humphrey was trying to develop a bond or at least a rapport with the southern conservative Democrats. After a while we walked out onto the grounds. Reporters milled around us and photographers jockeyed for position as we strolled. Several times the Vice-President casually draped his arm across my shoulders, while I just as casually managed to avoid the arm. He was walking to my left and, apparently determined to provide the photographers with a pose that indicated a narrowing of the gap between us, he put his right arm through the crook of my left in such a manner that I could not get out of it without seeming rude. The picture, featuring the famous Humphrey smile, appeared in newspapers all over the country the following day.

I was not particularly pleased at the implication that Lester Maddox had succumbed to the Humphrey charm and slipped toward the left. I had not (and *have* not and *will* not). I did take note of the fact that Mr. Humphrey, in a speech delivered later that day at the Lockheed Aircraft plant in nearby Marietta, addressed himself to the private enterprise system in America. Perhaps I had gotten through to him a bit after all.

As for our picture, I heard a little grumbling among some of my fellow conservatives. I also learned that Mr. Humphrey heard even more from the liberal radicals when he got back to Washington, and he even went so far as to deny it had happened until the picture was produced.

The effort to sway me was continued later at a governors' meeting at the White House. As I mingled with some forty-seven or forty-eight other governors in a room near the Oval Office, one of LBJ's special assistants took me aside and told me that the President would like for me to join him in the Oval Office. I was ushered in and LBJ shook my hand warmly.

"How about a drink, Governor Maddox?" and, apparently aware of my reputation as a teetotaler, added, "a Coke or a root beer?"

"A Coke will be just fine," I said.

He turned to the waiter standing nearby. "A Coke for the governor and a root beer for me."

We sat down and after the usual amenities, he said, "I'm looking forward to working with you."

"I appreciate that, Mr. President," I said. "You know, I've been here before, trying to work with you, but I couldn't get in." I reminded him of my picketing in the summer of 1964.

He smiled and nodded. "Oh yes, I remember."

"It's hard to work with your Administration. The trouble is, most of you national Democrats seem to think that if a man isn't radical or liberal, he can't be a Democrat. That kind of thinking lost you some ground in '66. Didn't the Democrats lose something like forty-seven House seats in those elections?"

He nodded, without the smile. "We sure did, Governor."

"And lost a governor in Arkansas and another in Florida. And if one of your liberal friends had been elected in Georgia the Democrats would probably have lost another five congressmen."

"I understand, Governor." He agreed that he had fought me in Georgia and that what I said was true.

"There's no doubt that your election did help hold onto some congressmen. Your election partially saved the South for the Democrats."

"But there's no conservative voice in the national party or in the Administration. In Georgia I've appointed men who opposed me and who differ politically with me because I think they're the best qualified men for the jobs they're in, and because their views represent the views of some of the citizens.

"We want to be your friend; we want to work with you," I went on, "but there's just no way we can go along with this socialism you call the Great Society program. You see, we've got a hat to hang up too, and we're ready to hang it up. But we need you to put up the hat rack."

He was sitting in his rocking chair. He took a sip of his root beer, rocking slowly and nodding. "I understand, Governor. We'll be doing our best to work with you."

We talked for a while longer but he never became specific, and when our meeting was over I was escorted back to where the other governors were. Almost at once another presidential aide approached me.

"Governor Maddox, would you please come with me? We're moving the group outside to the rose garden. If you go first, the others will follow you."

The request seemed peculiar, if for no other reason than the fact that politicians did not generally follow Lester Maddox. In fact, my experience had mostly been that I had to drag them along. Nevertheless, I went out the door he indicated, and as I glanced back to see if the others were following me, someone grasped my right hand firmly in a handshake, at the same time gripping my elbow with his other hand so that I could not draw back. I looked around and saw that it was President Johnson, whom I had just moments before left in the Oval Office. I also saw on the lawn one of the largest gatherings of television and news cameramen I had ever beheld. I had no choice but to submit to the prolonged handshake. Just as the picture in Atlanta with Hubert Humphrey, I sensed that this little tableau was designed to show that there was a rapport between conservative and liberal Democrats, for if Lester Maddox was seen standing alone with Lyndon Johnson, shaking hands, then we must have some understanding. I suppose I will never cease to be amazed by the ploys of some politicians.

After this meeting I found the White House easily accessible. I could call and get through to the President whenever necessary. During my campaigning I had told the voters that LBJ had been impounding highway funds, and that I would make an appeal to him to release these. He told me that he would have the situation examined, and although he made no firm commitment at the time, he said he would let me know.

Shortly after I got back to Georgia I received a message from Marvin Watson, Special Assistant to the President, advising that half the impounded funds would be released immediately and the remainder in thirty days. The Administration was trying to mend some fences.

Whatever his intentions at that meeting and others, a change in plan took place on March 31, 1968, when LBJ announced unequivocally, "I shall not seek, and I will not accept, the nomination of my party for another term as your President."

That news hardly had time to sink in on the nation when something of an even more disruptive character took place. On April 4, only four days after Johnson's dramatic announcement, Dr. Martin Luther King, Jr., was shot dead while standing on a motel balcony in Memphis, Tennessee. This immediately plunged the country into a crisis which made the rioting of recent years pall by comparison. President Johnson canceled a Vietnam strategy meeting in Hawaii even as his jet was being readied, and went on television less than an hour after Dr. King's death. He made an urgent plea to the people to reject the blind violence that had struck down Dr. King. But while he made this appeal to the nation, he knew what inevitably lay ahead. In his book *The Vantage Point,* LBJ wrote: "Perhaps the most disturbing thing about the April riots was the fact that so many of us almost instinctively expected them to happen as soon as the news of Dr. King's death was made known."

I did not agree with Lyndon Johnson on a great many political matters but I was in total accord on this. I had absolutely no reason to believe the rioting would stop short of Georgia and Martin Luther King's hometown of Atlanta, where the funeral would be held. On the contrary, I had every reason to believe otherwise. I felt then—and I feel now—that the man who fired the shot was merely an instrument. Dr. King's professed non-violent philosophy had bred violence. This was compounded rather than combated by the actions of the Kennedy and Johnson administrations. The proponents of violence, the Communists and other radical leftists, knew that Dr. King had outlived his usefulness to them, and he was now more valuable to them in death than in life. He was sacrificed not for the cause of freedom, but for the cause of anarchy.

My duty as governor of Georgia was clear: to prepare for the worst and hope for the best. The President himself, from the moment he spoke to the nation on television, was a virtual prisoner in the White House. The Secret Service reinforced the contingent guarding him and kept a helicopter in readiness on the grounds for immediate evacuation if it came to that. Within a matter of hours Washington was a scene of anarchy, terror, rioting, looting, burning, and murder. Of that night and the day that followed, Johnson wrote: "Inflammatory speeches filled the air; anger and bitterness fanned out. Wild rumors spread . . . I began to fear that once again the dangerous cycle had begun, and my fears came true. By the next day entire blocks of buildings were going up in smoke. Helmeted troops were patrolling the littered streets. Before the holocaust was over, forty other cities had experienced similar outbreaks from coast to coast."

The days that followed saw rioting at its worst. One hundred twenty-five cities were hit, at least forty-six people died violently, another 3,500 injured and maimed, arrests ran to 20,000, and this was minimized because in many places the rioters and looters went unmolested by the police. Insured property losses ran to more than $45,000,000, with untold uninsured property damage that had to be absorbed by the luckless owners.

Certain black leaders were making no secret of their intentions. Stokely Carmichael exhorted his followers: "We have to retaliate for the execution of Dr. King. Black people know that their way is not by intellectual discussion. They have to get guns. Our retaliation won't be in the courtroom, but in the streets of America."

Retaliation? Against whom? At that time the identity of the murderer was unknown.

Martin Luther King's funeral was to be held in Atlanta on Monday, April 8. Early estimates of from ten to thirty thousand people coming into the city for the funeral quickly escalated into a hundred thousand and more. The weekend was rife with tension. On Saturday night a band of black youths broke into a liquor store in downtown Atlanta, but Mayor Ivan Allen and his chief of police, Herbert Jenkins, apparently decided to make no effort to apprehend them for fear of touching off riots. The mayor stated that he was willing to "sacrifice" a couple of liquor stores. I cannot help but think of the owners of these "sacrificed" stores, and reflect upon how this sacrificial attitude toward individual rights in appeasing the mob has created the disrespect for law and order that has swept America.

My intention as governor was to examine the situation as calmly as possible, to weigh the intelligence coming to me from a number of sources, and to take whatever steps I felt to be absolutely necessary to protect the lives and property of the citizens of Georgia who looked to me for that protection. Troops of the Georgia National Guard, under Adjutant General George Hearn, were quietly stationed at strategic locations in the Atlanta area. One such contingent was even moved to another location when it was found that the funeral procession would pass close to its original position. In other words, these forces were in readiness for whatever might come, even though completely unobtrusive, not at all on the order of the troops moving about the city of Washington, D.C., in armored carriers.

The uncertainty of what might occur in Atlanta was vividly demonstrated when President Johnson expressed his desire to attend the funeral. Rufus W. Youngblood, Deputy Director of the Secret Service, relayed his feelings immediately to Johnson. "Absolutely not. The Secret Service feels this would place the President in a potentially dangerous situation." In his book *Twenty Years in the Secret Service,* Youngblood wrote:

We had reports that many militants, those who advocated violence, were urging blacks to take up arms and go into the streets in retaliation for the murder of King. Thousands of sympathizers, black and white, were already moving toward Atlanta from all over the country. The city would be packed, and we felt that a spark could touch off a condition in the Georgia capital that would make the previous weekend look like a picnic by comparison. The FBI added its weight in recommending strongly that the President not attend the funeral.

Against the protests of many of Atlanta's liberals, I kept the Capitol open on Monday. My political and philosophical differences with Martin Luther King were well known, and in view of this my attendance at the funeral would have been the grossest hypocrisy.

Although the Atlanta news media and the citizens of Georgia were not aware of it, among the intelligence that reached my office was a report that an attempt would be made to storm the Capitol building. I conferred with General Hearn and Colonel Harold Burson, the head of the Georgia State Patrol. It was decided that state troopers would be stationed inside the Capitol, but no National Guard troops.

Atlanta, as predicted, was filled to overflowing. Services were held at Ebenezer Baptist Church, where Dr. King and his father had been co-pastors, and then the funeral procession moved through the streets of the city toward the burial place. I watched as the mourners moved slowly past the Capitol in the wake of the mule-drawn wagon bearing the casket. Of the thousands of people I saw, I felt that most were there to express their love for their fallen leader. But there were many there out of far less lofty sentiments: would-be presidential hopefuls because they saw political expediency in it, many with the hope of stepping into the vacuum Dr. King's death had created in the civil rights movement, and unquestionably there were also those who intended turning this peaceful procession into a howling, destroying mob.

By the time 1968 rolled around, I thought I had been called just about everything that could be dreamed up by even the most rabid

anti-Maddox fanatic. I was wrong. A severe attack came from a
source I was accustomed to, the liberal media. The single word of
description they became fascinated with was "little." The mayor of
Atlanta, whose crystal ball did not tell him in advance whether the
city would come through unscathed or be turned into a raging bat-
tlefield, marched in the forefront of the procession and attempted
to dismiss me by stating that "Lester Maddox, of course, was cowering in the State Capitol . . . and there were rumors that he was
going to call up the National Guard for his protection."

The mayor was not quite right about that. The National Guard
was on duty and ready to protect the rights and property of all the
citizens, *including* Mayor Allen. It was true that word of the readiness of the Guard had been rumored, and it is not at all unlikely
that it was this news that deterred those who had threatened to
storm the Capitol. In my opinion, there can be little doubt that
these radicals would have taken advantage of the weakness of
what I considered Mayor Allen's "sacrificial" attitude, had they
thought such a man was in charge.

As to his allusion to my "cowering" in the State Capitol, I was
no more cowering in the Capitol than President Johnson was cowering in the White House. I do not doubt for a moment, though,
that there were a great many frightened people, of high position as
well as low, who were cowering in the procession that passed beneath my windows.

Lyndon Johnson, beaten by the war in Vietnam, a self-pro-
claimed lame duck more than seven months before the election, was
probably in no position to give Georgia more of the help he had
hinted at in our earlier meeting. Certainly I could not go along with
the ultra-liberals who moved in after Johnson dropped out. The
assassination of Bobby Kennedy scarcely two months after that of
Martin Luther King seemed to inflame the radical left to a fever
pitch.

As the National Democratic Convention grew nearer, there was
no conservative voice whatever being heard. With Kennedy gone,
there remained Humphrey, Eugene McCarthy, and George
McGovern, certainly a discouraging group for a conservative to
have to choose among.

I tried to express to the Democratic regional meeting in Atlanta, and again to the Platform Committee in Washington that it was essential for the party to move away from the free-wheeling liberalism and radicalism that had engulfed it. I predicted that the course they were on would cost the Democrats statehouses, congressional seats, and the White House. The Republicans had seldom had such bright prospects as the Democratic Party was providing it in the summer of 1968.

All hope of conservative participation in the platform had faded before the convention assembled in Chicago. I have never considered "going national," but I felt it urgent that someone make at least a last-ditch attempt to restore some sanity to a Democratic Party that was destroying itself. On August 17 I called a press conference at the Georgia Capitol and made an announcement.

> I am convinced that the problems which confront us are the direct result of our failure to insist that our leaders put first things first; the welfare of our children ahead of social experimentation; domestic needs ahead of foreign wishes; rights of individuals ahead of the whims of special interest groups; the safety of law-abiding citizens ahead of the safety of law-defying criminals; the American Democratic people ahead of the American Democratic Party.

> Like you I have waited for a Democrat to step forward who would fill the void that exists in the National Democratic Party. We have waited and waited and waited. Many of us have prayed. But the void has remained unfilled. I have been unable to find a representative of the conservative element of American society seeking the Democratic nomination for the highest office in our land.

> Now, having waited as long as conscience will allow me to wait, it is with the utmost personal humility, but still with great pride in, and love for, my country that I announce my intention to seek, with all possible vigor and determination, the Democratic nomination for the Presidency of the United States of America.

It was no snap decision to make this announcement. It was certainly no secret that Governor George Wallace, the American

Party candidate, was far and away my choice over any of the array of Democrats being prominently mentioned for the nomination. But I felt then that while the concept of an independent party is certainly to the overall advantage of the people, as a practicality at the national level, its chances of gaining office were virtually nil.

As titular head of the Democratic Party in Georgia I felt that I could not abandon the party. I even considered resigning as head of the Georgia delegation, but I did not do so as this might have wrecked the Georgia party.

So I left for Chicago, complete with a Secret Service detail, hopeful of being heard before the Platform Committee to make specific suggestions before it was too late. In Chicago I worked as hard as any candidate. For those who care to know, I made myself available as a candidate solely for this purpose, to try my very best to inject into the party and its nominees a little common sense and representation for the uncounted millions of conservatives all over the nation.

I never felt for an instant that my candidacy would meet with success, but I felt strongly that in failing I would cause the socialistic and power-mad politicians in charge of the national party and under the influence of the beatniks, hippies, political parasites, and other unsavory types to react in such a manner as to let all of America see how ugly, prejudiced, cowardly, and deceitful the leadership of our national Democratic Party was. In that sense, my effort was a success.

Chapter 11

Stepping Down

Nearing the end of my term, I made an inventory of the things I had set out to do and the things that had actually been accomplished. Thank God, because of the support of the people— Democrats and Republicans, black and white, rich and poor—we were able to get more private citizens involved in their state government than in the rest of the twentieth century combined. The prophets of doom had been proven wrong. The honesty, efficiency, and morality in government that I had promised had become fact. Where my opponents had predicted economic disaster, we could now look back over four years that brought more dollars for new and expanded industry to Georgia than in the entire sixteen years prior to that. It had taken more than a century to bring Georgia's budget for higher education to an annual level of $71 million. During the Maddox administration it soared to $159 million, and it was reported that it was a higher percentage increase than in any other state during that same period. Elementary and secondary education made advances that were not only greater than at any other time in the state's history, but greater than during the two previous administrations combined. Teachers' salaries were increased to the extent that we were able to attract and keep good teachers. Vocational and technical school facilities were expanded more than ever before. The first real penal reform was begun, and mental health programs and facilities saw greater advances than at any other time.

The momentum of these and other programs and promises was still carrying them on and I felt strongly that this momentum could be maintained and increased through another four-year Maddox term.

There was, however, a major obstacle to this. The Georgia Constitution, in the form adopted in 1945, declared the incumbent governor ineligibile for succession to that office during the four years immediately following his term in office. I discussed this with my legal aide, Frank Blankenship, as well as with several other attorneys. The decision was reached to file suit to test the constitutionality of such a restriction. The office of governor was the only elective position—state or local—in Georgia subject to such a prohibition, and only a few other states had such a law. It seemed to be an obvious violation of my rights and the rights of those who supported me.

The suit was filed by Tully Bond, a Macon attorney, and although it was carried all the way to the U. S. Supreme Court, to my surprise the law was not overturned. It was final. It was the law, and I was obliged to abide by it. I could not run for governor in 1970.

A similar situation had developed in Alabama, where it was obvious the people wanted George Wallace to continue as their governor. As in Georgia, state law prohibited him from doing so. The Wallace family remained in the governor's mansion by the simple expedient of Mrs. Lurleen Wallace running and handily overcoming her opposition.

I considered asking Virginia to do the same thing, but the more I thought of it, the more I realized I could not ask her to undergo the stress and strain of being the central figure in a political campaign or of facing the rigorous duties of the office itself. I knew that if I asked her, she would do it; therefore the idea was discarded.

I was receiving thousands of requests—by telephone, mail, and in person—to remain in state government. The obvious position, if I chose to become a candidate, was the office of lieutenant governor. I had stated some time earlier that I would not seek this office. Quite frankly, at the time I made this statement I was completely confident that the restriction on my succeeding myself as governor would be easily struck down as unconstitutional.

The time had come for me to re-evaluate my decision. Financially, I would be taking a considerable cut. The governor's salary was $42,000, and there was the mansion and an additional $25,000 household allowance with which to operate it. In contrast to that, the lieutenant governor received a salary of $20,000. But as practical as money is, I had not gotten into politics for money and even though I had no other income at the time, this drastic cut was not one of the considerations as to whether to run or not. Virginia and I and our family had managed on far less than $20,000.

The campaign itself was something to be considered. A political campaign for a statewide office is virtually a full-time occupation in itself, and as governor I already had a full-time job. If I ran, my campaign activities would have to be limited.

On the other side of the scales was the fact that as lieutenant governor I would have an official position from which to help keep alive the work of the previous four years, a forum from which I could be heard and from which I could exert a positive influence on the direction of state government.

I weighed both sides, made my decision, and announced my candidacy. No other Georgia governor had done this. In fact, to my knowledge, only one other governor in the South had tried it, and that was Governor Paul Johnson, of Mississippi, and he was soundly defeated.

There were four Democrats in the race; incumbent Lieutenant Governor George T. Smith, Democratic House Whip Carlie M. Jones, Mr. D. F. Glover, and myself.

As usual, the gubernatorial race attracted a swarm of candidates. There were three Republicans and nine Democrats. Former Governor Carl Sanders (whom I had succeeded), a moderate, and State Senator Jimmy Carter, a liberal, were considered to be the front runners among the Democrats, and due to the size of the field it was almost a foregone conclusion that these two would wind up in a runoff.

There was one candidate, Mr. J. B. Stoner, an avowed white racist who was, to put it as charitably as I can, absolutely without tact in his public utterances. I recall one speaking engagement in Waynesboro at which the candidates for governor and lieutenant governor had been invited to address the people. When it came Mr. Stoner's turn at the podium he launched into his usual tirade against what he called "niggers and Jews."

I listened in amazement and disgust for a moment, hardly believing my ears even though I had been told this was his manner when speaking. I turned to the man seated next to me and whispered, "I can't take any more of this!"

"I agree with you, Governor," he whispered back.

"I'm leaving!" I said, and I got up and began to walk off the speakers' platform. It was like pulling the plug in a bathtub. There was a sudden stampede behind me and I was almost knocked off my feet as the other candidates poured off the platform, each not wishing to be the last to leave.

On September 9 the voters went to the polls to nominate their party's candidates. Even though I had little opportunity to campaign actively I won a clear victory over the incumbent and two other opponents, without a runoff, as I had predicted.

As had been generally expected, Carl Sanders and Jimmy Carter went into a runoff for the Democratic gubernatorial nomination. I suddenly found myself to be a very popular man with both camps. Senator Gene Holley, campaign co-ordinator for Governor Sanders, arranged a meeting between us soon after the primary returns were conclusive. Carl Sanders was seeking my endorsement to his candidacy, and he was doing so in all propriety. But in the course of our conversation he brought up something that I had never before considered.

"I want you to know," he told me, "that as governor I'll never try to interfere with your office or with the business of the Senate. I will not use my power or influence as governor to direct the election of the president pro tem, or any Senate committee chairman or committee member. You have my solemn word on that."

I was both amazed and dismayed by the implication. Never once during my years as governor had I so much as called a member of the House or Senate or made even a veiled suggestion as to who should be elected to any legislative office or appointed to any committee. This was the job and responsibility of the legislative branch. His remarks indicated that purpose and practice had not necessarily coincided in this vital area of separation of powers of the branches of state government. This was not naïveté on my part, but simply a strong belief in constitutional procedure.

I had respect for the function of the legislature. During my administration that body had achieved the greatest degree of in-

25, 26. Campaign '74.

27, 28, 29, 30. Campaign '74.

dependence in recent Georgia history. I worked for this independence. My refusal to resort to strong-arm tactics, threats, rewards, dealings in smoke-filled rooms, and other time-tested methods of subverting the constitutionally intended powers and functions of the legislature was misinterpreted by my critics as an indication of weakness on my part. Nothing could have been further from the truth. The real effectiveness of the Maddox administration was due in great measure to my taking my programs before the people. If the people of Georgia found them to have merit, they would let their legislators know it. Too many men who have occupied that office have bypassed the people entirely, and in doing so have lost touch with the very force which put them into office. The man who succeeded me is one of the most flagrant examples of this that I have seen.

I thanked Governor Sanders for his reassurances and I told him that I could not publicly endorse a candidate in the governor's—or any other—race. This was my belief and my practice. When I had seen him out, I walked out onto the porch and told Virginia what had taken place at the meeting.

"I want to find out what the other candidates have to say on this particular subject," I said. I sat down in a rocker and gazed off across the green lawn. "I think we'll just sit back and wait."

We did not have to wait long. Mr. David Gambrell, Jimmy Carter's campaign manager, called me and arranged for a meeting with his candidate. They came to the mansion and after we had talked of his campaign for a few minutes, I brought up the subject of the Senate and the role of the lieutenant governor as the presiding officer of that body.

Mr. Carter came directly to the point. "I don't intend interfering with the lieutenant governor," he said, "but, of course, I do expect to have a voice in naming committee chairmen and committee members."

I looked at him in complete disbelief, and I realized at that moment how important it was that Governor Sanders had brought this up.

"Senator Carter," I said, "if that's your intention, I want you to know I look on it as an intrusion on the constitutional powers of the lieutenant governor, as well as an intrusion on the express wishes of the people who elect him to office."

He seemed to sense immediately the strength of my beliefs and he altered his position slightly, indicating that he would not interfere in the naming of the committee members, but that he *did* intend to have a say in the naming of chairmen.

Mr. Carter could not have made his intention for the next four years any clearer than by the statements he made to me that day. Unlike Governor Sanders, who had voluntarily brought up the matter and voluntarily assured me of non-interference, Senator Carter, when faced with a direct question, had informed me unequivocally that he did plan such interference. To me the effect of this, if he succeeded, would have been to set up a virtual dictatorship with the executive branch controlling the legislature, a clear violation of the intent of the state's Constitution.

Prior to the runoff between Sanders and Carter, I placed an ad, at my own personal expense, in newspapers around the state, calling on them, as well as Republican candidate Hal Suit, to make public, for the record, their positions on gubernatorial interference with the functioning of the legislature. All responded that they definitely would *not* interfere or involve themselves in any way in this sort of activity.

This public statement of Mr. Carter's was the exact opposite of what he had demanded when he met with me in the presence of his campaign director, Mr. Gambrell. Unfortunately, as time went by this sort of thing proved to be the rule rather than the exception with Mr. Carter.

Shortly after this, Jimmy Carter won the Democratic primary runoff. In the month and a half between this and the November general election, he worked almost as hard against Lester Maddox as he did against his Republican opponent.

As a political expedient, Carter—as well as Mr. Suit—launched an attack on a man who had long been a controversial figure in Georgia politics, Mr. Jim Gillis, the venerable highway commissioner. In years gone by, I must admit I had come to believe some of the things I read about "Mr. Jim" and had concluded that there might be more than a little rascality in him. But as governor I had found this impression to be wrong; I found him to be an extremely able adminstrator, a dedicated man serving in public office not for money or a livelihood, but because he knew and loved his job and had respect for the taxpayers whose funds were entrusted to him. Inevitably over the years he had stepped on many toes.

Consequently, when Carter and others continued to heap abuse on "Mr. Jim," I made up my mind to speak out in his defense. As this became known around my office, I was strongly advised to leave it alone, that it was politically dangerous to take on an unpopular cause. But I have always felt that truth is more important than political expediency, and I did not like the character assassination that Mr. Gillis and his family were having to endure. My family and I had experienced it ourselves, and I knew the anguish it caused from firsthand experience.

I told my press secretary to call a press conference. "Tell them that Lester Maddox is going to tell them the truth about Jim Gillis."

Reporters and cameramen came on the run. I discovered later that they had come expecting me, at this eleventh hour in the campaign, to jump on the bandwagon and denounce the longtime highway commissioner. When I came out strongly in defense of Jim Gillis, they were amazed.

During this same period I announced that state revenues were on the decline due to the general national economic slowdown, and I called on department heads to cut back spending for the remainder of the year.

Both these things, considered only from the point of view of political strategy, were obviously not in the best interest of my own candidacy. But even with this, and the limited time—hardly three full days—that I was able to spend on the campaign trail, in the general election I emerged victorious over my Republican opponent, Frank Miller, with almost 74 per cent of the vote.

As expected, Jimmy Carter won over Hal Suit.

Carter, confident of his ultimate victory, had never slackened his efforts to line up votes in the Senate by making commitments, pledges, promises, and bringing pressure to bear in any way he could on as many senators as he could. All this despite his public denunciation of such an effort to control the Senate.

Outgoing Lieutenant Governor George T. Smith aligned himself with the Carter forces with the intention of calling a caucus soon after Carter's victory in November. Apparently, they felt they had sufficient power to name Carter's handpicked man to the job of president pro tem of the Senate. The meeting was officially scheduled, but they soon found they had acted hastily. Carter did not have the backing of as many senators as he had thought, and since there was no way that the meeting could be canceled, a change of strategy was made. Lieutenant Governor Smith would call the meeting to order, a motion to adjourn would be made and seconded, and the meeting adjourned, thus avoiding the crucial vote.

Senator Gene Holley, however, alert and in good voice, made himself so insistent that Lieutenant Governor Smith had no choice but to recognize him. Given the floor, Senator Holley moved that the caucus proceed with the election of the president pro tem. The Carter forces were thwarted; Senator Hugh Gillis won the post, and an otherwise inevitable power struggle in January was averted. It was a case, as the old saying goes, of being hoist by one's own petard.

This was pictured by the news media as a victory for Lester Maddox and a defeat for Jimmy Carter. I looked on it simply as a victory for the people and for representative government, and a strong setback for those with dictatorial aspirations.

Thus, even before either of us took office, Jimmy Carter and I were billed in the press as adversaries. All my adult life I had been an outspoken proponent of the constitutional separation of the executive, legislative, and judicial branches of government. As governor I had worked for legislative independence as probably no governor before me had done, and I did not intend to stand by as lieutenant governor in silence and without a fight as one man attempted to destroy that independence. My fight was not against the man himself, but against all who would work against representative government. I had promised the people in my campaign that I would stand firmly against dishonesty, inefficiency, and special interest, and that no matter who became their governor, if I saw him doing wrong, I would tell on him.

Soon after the general election, Carter announced his intention to reorganize the state government. For all the high-sounding purpose, governmental reorganization such as Carter intended has, in every case I have studied, wound up with more bureaucracy, more money expended, and less efficiency than the government that was there prior to the reoganization.

A wedge was found in an issue that had been festering for quite some time in the minds of many legislators and other constitutional officers and state officials: the issue of a salary increase and increased pension benefits.

This is always a sore subject, for regardless of the merits of salary increases, no one wants to be identified as being in favor of it. Legislators have to legislate their own pay raises and whether it is justified or not, there is strong reluctance for fear of criticism by their constituents and the inevitability of an opponent making political hay of it in the next election.

Out of the determination of the governor to get his reorganization legislation enacted, and out of the frustration of some legislative leaders and others who were just as determined to see a salary bill passed but who did not want their names attached to it, it appeared to me that a "deal" was hatched.

Publicly, Governor Carter remained aloof from the salary bill, and some of its proponents were opposed to his plan of reorganization. The two sides were, in effect, saying to each other: "You scratch my back, and I'll scratch yours." It was the classic back-room, secret, self-serving sort of thing engaged in by some politicians which tends to give a bad name to all.

The "deal" involved having both these controversial measures legislated by a method known as the "reverse veto," a clearly illegal and unconstitutional device in which the legislative branch surrenders to the executive branch its authority and responsibility to enact and repeal legislation. It is a proper function of the governor to formulate legislation and have it introduced into the legislature by his floor leaders. In the "reverse veto," however, the proposed legislation is not only introduced, but by prearrangement the legislature then must *veto* it or it automatically becomes law.

To give an example, the Georgia House of Representatives is comprised of 180 members. In the proper course of action, if ninety-one members are present during a vote (ninety-one being a quorum), all ninety-one would have to vote *for* a bill in order for it to pass. By the "reverse veto," on the other hand, all ninety-one would have to vote *against* the bill or it would automatically become law. In addition, the Georgia Supreme Court had ruled on previous occasions that it was illegal for the General Assembly to delegate to others its constitutional authority to pass laws. In my opinion, Governor Carter, the House leadership, the state Law Department, and other state leaders knew of this constitutional question, but they were willing to take a chance in the hope that no one would call their hand on this "deal."

This "deal" was giving Governor Carter dictatorial powers in return for his seeing to it that the salary increases went through. It was kept secret from me, obviously because the participants knew me well enough to realize I would blow the whistle on them.

Actually, I had every hope of being able to work harmoniously with Governor Carter. During the period between the general election and the taking of office, I did everything I could to make the transition as smooth as possible for Jimmy Carter. I recall all too vividly the time during which I was governor-elect—only a matter of minutes, actually—and I felt it incumbent upon me to do whatever I could to make it easier for this governor than it had been for me. It was only common sense that this was in the best interest of Georgia.

As it turned out, I was in for a shock. Shortly after assuming office, the governor sent word that he would like to see me. This meeting, incidentally, was destined to be the first of only two or three private meetings between us throughout the entire four years that followed. I went to his office, where we chatted amicably for a few minutes. I assured him that I was looking forward to working with him and supporting him in every possible way to keep Georgia moving forward.

"I appreciate that," Governor Carter said, "and I want all the support I can get. But I didn't call you in here to find out where and how you're going to support me. I called you here to tell you that if you ever oppose me on *any* issue I'll meet you head on and fight you with all the resources under my command and authority."

I was absolutely dumbfounded! No one had ever spoken to me quite like that before. "Governor Carter," I said, "you shock me! I don't want to fight you; in fact, I sincerely hope we can avoid that.

If it comes down to a fight, then you'll have to initiate it. But I can assure you that if you do, I'll be compelled to fight back!"

His background as a submarine commander had been well publicized, and I could not help but see him as he stood there, the ultimate authority, telling me: *I am the commander of this ship! All others are secondary and subservient to me!* It brought to mind his earlier demands when we met at the mansion during the campaign. It was not a face he would ever reveal to the public, but he was making it very clear that if I would not be his puppet, he would do his level best to destroy me.

Perhaps this ultimatum—for what else could it be called? —would not have come as such a shock to me if it had taken place after I learned of the "deal." News of that reached me first during the 1971 session of the legislature, in January. Before I could react, word was quickly sent to me from the state Law Department via my legal aide, Frank Blankenship, that if I went along with them on greasing the ways for the passage of a Salary Commission Bill, the salary of the lieutenant governor would be raised by as much as $10,000 or $15,000 a year. The legislating of the salary increases was to work this way: The Salary Commission Bill, to be introduced without my knowledge, would call for the appointment of a commission comprised of businessmen from various sectors of the state. If the Salary Commission Bill introduced by Representative George Busbee and others had been railroaded through the Senate as it was through the House, and the salary increases would hopefully become law during the 1971 session of the General Assembly, this commission would then have a period of only thirty days in which to have its members appointed, organize itself and its staff, conduct a study of salary structures in the federal government, other state governments, as well as in private business and industry, digest this mass of material, and arrive at a schedule of salary increases for legislators, judges, department heads, and many others. These recommendations would automatically become law *unless* the legislature voted them down via the "reverse veto."

In addition to the obvious impossibility of accomplishing all this within thirty days, the intent clearly was to solve this sticky problem in such a way as to relieve the individual legislators of any blame for its enactment.

There were many in state government who were five, six, or more years overdue for a pay increase, but to wrap it all up in one big bundle in which the deserving and undeserving alike received increases in a way that one could not get it without the other, was absolutely against the public interest. And the attempt to have such ill-conceived legislation passed by the "reverse veto" made it all the worse.

My reaction was immediate and strong. I used every means at my disposal to expose this shady "deal" to the public and to uninformed members of the legislature. Governor Carter had initiated a fight, and, as I had told him, I was compelled to fight back.

The Salary Commission Bill was introduced into the House, where it quickly passed. Thanks to the support of my position by many senators, it was just as quickly defeated in its original form when it reached the Senate. An amended version was passed before the 1971 session adjourned, omitting the "reverse veto" provision. This was a major victory for me and those who supported my view. Now, when the commission presented its recommendations, a positive vote would have to be taken, not the backdoor and illegal route of "reverse veto." These recommendations were not forthcoming by the time the session ended, for the bill was delayed in the Senate for a long period of time and there was no salary increase in 1971.

The increase was obviously high on Governor Carter's list of priorities as the 1972 session of the General Assembly drew near. The Salary Commission had made its study and had its recommendations ready to present to the legislature. In December 1971, a few weeks before the legislature was to convene, members of the commission came to me in an effort to gain my support for passage of their recommendations. I was shown the figures—which included a $10,000 annual pay hike for the lieutenant governor. In almost every instance, the figures I saw were nearly identical to what I learned had been privately circulated by the proponents of the Salary Bill before the bill was introduced to appoint a group of citizens to recommend what the politicians wanted but did not have the guts to ask for.

I told them that they were being used in a very shoddy way by the men who had concocted this "deal" more than a year ago, and that as long as attempts to ram through salary increases in this package fashion were made, I would steadfastly oppose them. I told them that if specific increases were needed, such as judges, department heads, legislators, or any other office, then a bill specifying the particular position should be introduced. If I were convinced the need was legitimate, then I would support it wholeheartedly.

The administration was committed, however, to hold up its end of the "deal," and the Salary Commission recommendations were presented in the House when the General Assembly convened. In the absence of a recorded roll call vote in the House of Representatives they were overwhelmingly approved. While we in the Senate had been successful in knocking out the "reverse veto," there still remained a way to pass the salary increases while at the same time relieving the individual legislators of personal blame, and that was by a voice vote or show of hands. A roll call vote, on the other hand, indelibly inscribes each man's vote on the record for everyone to see. Georgia law provides in both House and Senate that if a motion is made for a roll call vote, and if 20 per cent of those voting are in favor of the motion, a roll call vote must be taken.

When the bill again reached the Senate in 1972, a motion for a roll call vote was made and passed, and the bill was defeated by a vote of fifty-five to zero. Although there was no mention of it in the liberal pro-Carter anti-Maddox media, this victory of the lieutenant governor and the Senate over two consecutive efforts to slip this ill-conceived bill through the legislature effected a savings of more than $4 million for the taxpayers of Georgia.

Governor Carter's controversial Reorganization Bill *was* legislated in 1972 by the "reverse veto." But our fight the previous year which had eliminated this trick in relation to the Salary Bill had raised doubt. The Salary Bill was being tested in the courts, and the Carter forces quickly moved to have all the reorganization provisions included in an "omnibus" bill, and it was in this manner that they finally passed both houses and become law. Fear of the "reverse veto" bill that had been passed forced them to abide by the Georgia Constitution.

We—meaning those of us in favor of conducting the government in a constitutional manner and of enacting legislation without resorting to trickery and backroom "deals"—had them with their backs against the wall, and they knew it.

Nevertheless, in December of 1972, as the 1973 General Assembly session approached, I was again approached by members of the Salary Commission and urged to change my stand. I was, they told me, the only statewide elected official who stood in its way. In an apparent effort to soften my position they proposed *lowering* the proposed increase of my salary from $10,000 to $5,000. I told them again that my position on a package, across-the-board sort of increase was precisely what it had always been. I was opposed to it and would do everything in my power to keep it from passing.

It was certainly no secret that the governor was in a tight spot. Reorganization had become fact, and now those with whom he had made the "deal" were looking to him to deliver. Throughout the months since the adjournment of the 1972 legislative session, much pressure had been brought to bear on a great many legislators. Now, with the 1973 General Assembly convened, he could no longer maintain the aloofness he had publicly shown toward the Salary Bill. Pulling back this veil of secrecy, Governor Carter instructed his floor leaders, Senator Al Holloway and Senator Hugh Carter (a cousin), to introduce the measure. The Carter administration, the governor's floor leaders, and others, had worked long and hard behind the scenes to stave off a roll call vote, and on February 20, it came to a vote.

Not unexpectedly, a senator made a motion for a roll call vote. As required of me under the Georgia Constitution and the rules of the Senate, I called for a vote on the motion. The motion again passed, the roll was called, and the Salary Bill once more met a stone wall in the Senate.

The shock of this third consecutive defeat must have been considerable to Governor Carter. Senator Holloway served notice that he would move for reconsideration of the measure at the proper time. Interviewed by reporters, the senator stated that he was confident the measure would pass if a roll call vote could be avoided.

The following morning, February 21, when I arrived at the Capitol Senator Mike Padgett came to me. "I have been advised this morning, through the governor's floor leadership, that they do not expect a roll call vote on reconsideration," he said. "However, if there is such a motion and there's any doubt at all about the required vote, they're going to challenge you."

I thanked Senator Padgett for bringing me this information. As presiding officer of the Senate, I had never been challenged on a vote. Governor Carter, as he had threatened shortly after taking office, was meeting me head on and fighting me with all the resources at his command.

At the prescribed hour I called the Senate to order. As expected, Senator Holloway made his motion for reconsideration of the Salary Bill. Senator Mike Heardon immediately rose and made a motion for a roll call vote. Adhering strictly to the Senate rules, I acknowledged his motion and said:

"All those in favor rise, stand, and be counted!"

The words were a formality as a scattering of hands went up. The secretary of the Senate tallied the hands.

"All those opposed!" I said.

Again, the secretary and his staff made the count. "Eight in favor," he announced. "Thirty-one opposed."

More than the required 20 per cent had voted in favor of the motion. "The secretary will proceed with the roll call," I instructed.

There was a sudden clamor from the floor as the governor's floor leaders and others challenged the vote count, just as Senator Padgett had said they intended doing under these circumstances. It is not unusual to call for verification concerning a roll call vote, and under the threat that had been made it was imperative to make the verification.

I again called for the ayes and nays; the secretary and his staff carefully counted the hands.

More votes had been cast this time. "Seven in favor," the secretary said, "thirty-six opposed."

The thing I had fought against successfully for over two years had now happened. The motion for the roll call vote had failed by a scant two votes. As presiding officer, I could do only that which the law required of me. On numerous other occasions I had called for a roll call vote without a motion by one of the senators in order to get a quorum on the floor, and at other times when I felt it important for the senators' votes to be recorded. This time, however,

I was prohibited from doing so, for a senator quickly made the roll call vote motion. As a motion on the floor it *had* to be voted upon. At this time no presiding officer could legally override the vote of the Senate. The Georgia Senate had declined a roll call vote and with a heavy heart I called for a show of hands on reconsideration of the Salary Bill. The result, as Senator Holloway had so confidently said to the press earlier, was predictable. The motion carried, and the "deal" born in iniquity more than two years earlier was at last completed. Governor Carter had finally fulfilled his commitment to help the Salary Bill in exchange for the passage of his reorganization legislation. It stood as a glowing example of government by, of, and for the special interest crowd.

I had done everything I could to prevent this taking place. But now that it had happened, despite the concerted efforts of myself and others, the strangest thing of all occurred. The Carter forces, some politicians who were afraid to admit their own guilt, and the liberal-radical news media were saying that Lester Maddox was to blame for the Salary Bill!

I had fought it with all my strength up until—and including— the final vote. I sincerely believed that my constant efforts to disclose to the public what was being attempted would bring enough pressure to bear on the members of the legislature by the voters to assure that the bill would not pass, with or without a roll call vote. On that final day I had conducted the vote precisely as was called for by the Georgia Constitution and the Rules of the Senate. To have called for a roll call vote at this time, after the Senate had voted otherwise, would have put me in direct conflict with the constitution and the Senate rules.

Purposefully ignored amid all the propaganda that I had allowed the bill to pass, was the important fact that the bill *still* had to pass the House—which it did—and it *still* had to cross Governor Carter's desk without a veto—which it also did. Had it not passed in the House and been signed into law by the governor, it would not be the law today.

This incident stands as the grossest example of cowardly politicians pushing through special interest legislation that I have had the misfortune to witness. In combination with the biased liberal news media, these men perpetrated a cover-up even more dishonest than the Watergate scandal. The people of Georgia deserve better than shoddy deals conceived behind closed doors by politicians who do not have the guts to admit their own guilt when they are caught.

Midway through my first term as governor the legislature had passed an amendment to the 1965 act which had created the Metropolitan Atlanta Rapid Transit Authority (MARTA). As a native Atlantan I was well aware of the importance and essential need for a rapid transit system. But there were priorities involving the Atlanta freeways that were being overlooked and there were a number of things about the amendments that deeply disturbed me. The amendment called for the elimination of competitive bidding on the bond issue if sufficiently low rates were not achieved. This would result in negotiated bidding, which could tempt collusion and cost the taxpayers millions of dollars.

The officials of MARTA were saying that the estimated cost of the system was $385 million, but they could not come up with concrete evidence to substantiate this figure. When I suggested it would be more like $1 *billion* I was ridiculed for mentioning such a huge figure, and accused of being anti-rapid transit.

Something else that bothered me was the proposal of an ad valorem tax on the citizens of the metropolitan counties that would participate in the system. This was grossly unfair, in my view, as the property owners who would be footing the bill would, as a general rule, be the last to benefit from the system.

The pressure to go ahead with MARTA was tremendous, with caution literally thrown to the winds. The cost of the system to the taxpayers appeared to be of little or no concern to its promoters. The unanswered questions were overwhelming in their long-range implications. There were no accurate and reliable estimates of the cost of acquisitions of land, fees for engineering and financial consultants, and numerous other items.

A situation had already arisen in San Francisco with BART where costs had skyrocketed to more than $1.5 billion, forcing a vote on additional bonds. If this were to happen with MARTA, and if the voters were disenchanted by promises that had not been met and voted down the issue, we could wind up with an investment of $6 to $8 hundred million in a white elephant that would never be completed.

The amendment also put MARTA into the business of relocating housing and businesses displaced by the system, a function for which MARTA was not qualified. Even worse, through MARTA and federal aid, the federal government would have taken over the planning and development of much of metropolitan Atlanta, removing this from the hands of local citizens and their local governments, where it rightfully belongs.

The bill had powerful supporters: city and county administrations, big banks, large property owners, the Atlanta Newspapers, television, and radio—in short, the establishment. Somebody in the midst of all this pressure had to look out for the interests of the people who were being asked to sign a blank check. I had run for office on the promise that I would protect these interests. In keeping with this promise, I had no choice but to veto the bill, which I did.

In late 1970 the subject of rapid transit again became a prominent issue. Fortunately, even though I was serving out the last days of my term as governor, I was coming into office as lieutenant governor. I was still in a position to effectively oppose amendments to the MARTA act if attempts were made to push them through in the same form that had been tried in 1968. I was completely in favor of rapid transit, but I could lend my support only if it were handled with more fiscal responsibility than I had seen demonstrated up until that time.

Sophisticated Madison Avenue techniques were applied, with the suggestion of urgency and a tone of "we need it at any cost."

The ad valorem tax approach was abandoned in favor of a local option sales tax, which was to be applied in the participating counties over and above the statewide 3 per cent tax. This, at least, was a move in the right direction.

The first proposal was for a tax of 0.5 per cent. When no opposition was heard to this, it was then proposed that the tax be set at 0.75 per cent with the additional 0.25 per cent going toward subsidizing the fares.

Federal funds were to provide not less than two thirds the construction cost of the system, and the original legislation provided that the state of Georgia would be obligated for up to 10 per cent of these costs.

It was now suggested that the sales tax be set at 1 per cent, this latest 0.25 per cent increase being designed to relieve the state of the obligation for its share of construction costs.

I began to do some figuring. If the cost were to come to $1 billion, that meant that Georgia was obligated for $100 million, or 10 per cent. The estimated revenue from a 1 per cent sales tax for a period of fifty years was $25.8 billion. One fourth of this was $6.45 billion. In other words, in order to save the state $100 million, the promoters of this scheme were proposing a tax burden of $6.45 billion!

Governor Carter, as well as many others of the statehouse political establishment stood foursquare behind it. The special interests who stood to gain financially and otherwise by this unprecedented flood of tax dollars had exerted such pressure that the statehouse "go-along-with-anything" crowd adopted the proposal—knowingly or possibly unwittingly—without raising any objection to the built-in waste and misuse of billions of dollars belonging to the taxpayers of Georgia.

As lieutenant governor I asked the legal and financial leaders of MARTA, legislative and local government leaders, and others promoting the 1 per cent sales tax just what they were going to do with all this money. "We really had no idea so much money would be collected," was their response, and they insinuated doubt as to the accuracy of my figures. Here we had some of Atlanta's business and professional leaders, and state and local government leaders either admitting they did not know what was going on, or else they had been caught and would not admit their determination to push through rapid transit to provide for their own and other selfish and special interests, regardless of cost.

To my further amazement they responded: "We really don't know what we're going to do with all this money." To me they sounded more like children in their early school years than grown men recognized as leaders in business, the professions, and government.

One of the most astonishing responses of all came from Atlanta Mayor Sam Massell. I knew that rapid transit would certainly be beneficial to the metropolitan Atlanta area, but building it should not be used as an excuse to waste billions of tax dollars. I wanted to know what benefits others thought would be gained from building the system, and I asked Mayor Massell his views on this. He replied: "I really don't know how much good rapid transit itself will do for Atlanta, but I do know that spending that kind of money will have a great impact on the city."

What they were asking of the people of the five-county metropolitan area (only two counties ultimately chose to participate in the system) were taxes amounting to more money than the states of Georgia and Alabama *combined* had spent on all government functions from their beginning to the present time! And more than Louisiana, Mississippi, Alabama, Georgia, Florida, North and South Carolina, Tennessee, Virginia, and Arkansas had expended in their entire history on the paving of highways! This is precisely the sort of muddled thinking that drains the producers and hard workers of America.

They asked me what I would agree to that would allow me to stop fighting them.

"Instead of 1 per cent sales tax with no time limit, have it for the first ten years, then reduce it to 0.5 per cent," I told them. I also proposed that the fare should reflect operating cost by requiring that the fare each year be set at a figure based on one half the actual operating cost of the previous year. Thus bureaucrats and politicians who would otherwise have no restraint on them would hear from the public whenever operating costs tended to get out of hand.

While these figures of 0.25 per cent and 0.5 per cent appear small, in actuality they are astronomical in terms of dollars. My insistence on this reduction after ten years, for example, amounted to a savings to the taxpayers of $12.6 billion over the period between the tenth and fiftieth year of operation; as much as Georgia had spent for all of state government for the ninety-year period from 1881 to 1970.

These concessions to common sense were made. If I had not voiced opposition to these things, MARTA would have been allowed to proceed with the original plans. Governor Carter was so incensed by my opposition that shortly thereafter he called for the abolition of the office of lieutenant governor. The radical-liberal press began to play the same tune, as did a number of politicians who had long since learned that attacking Lester Maddox was about the only sure way to get their names in the papers.

It was another glaring attempt at government by "deal," where legislation is passed that contains some obvious good, but where no one takes it upon himself to look closely enough to point out what might be wrong, or what special interests are being served.

Chapter 12

Campaign 1974: Government by Deal

Since the 1940s, when the law was changed in Georgia preventing a governor from succeeding himself in that office it has become almost axiomatic that once a man is out, he stays out. Marvin Griffin, Ellis Arnall, Ernest Vandiver, Herman Talmadge, and Carl Sanders all failed to make it back.

I was well aware of this, and I had learned a great many things about political campaigns and government by the time 1974 rolled around and I entered my final year as lieutenant governor. The traditional Maddox-haters were saying that my candidacy was a foregone conclusion, and that I was simply using my present office as a launching pad. This, of course, was not the case at all. My personal desire was *not* to run. Eight years in the two top state elective offices had been a trying time for me, a burden on my health, my finances, and, most important of all, on my family

On the one hand there had been the joy and satisfaction of accomplishment, of seeing progressive, honest, and open government during my time as governor, and of having a forum from which to speak out and take effective action in protecting the interests of the people while lieutenant governor.

On the other hand there had been the torment and frustration of not being able to root out all the hypocrisy and dishonesty that seems to sprout endlessly in government, like weeds in a garden. There was the added irritation of being under constant attack by the liberal-radical media in editorials, cartoons, and even so-called news coverage, simply because their narrow view could see no good in a man who did not agree with their philosophy and over whom they exercised no control.

I knew that the powerful forces I had fought against during those years were no longer as splintered as they had been in previous elections when it came to working for the defeat of Lester Maddox. I felt strongly, however, that in a second term as governor I would be able to continue successfully my fight for decent, honest, open, moral government.

A great many friends and supporters from all across Georgia were encouraging me to announce my candidacy. I counseled with close friends and associates, and, as always, I discussed plans for the future with Virginia. I knew that deep down in her heart she longed for the relative tranquillity of private life, but she did not try to sway me. And I prayed—not for God to give me an answer, but as I always had prayed, for Him to use me as He saw fit. The answer would have to be mine, and it was not an easy decision to reach.

I had not lined my pockets, as far too many men in political life do, and Virginia and I had been "moonlighting" during my term as lieutenant governor by operating a small shop in Underground Atlanta. We opened only at night, after I concluded my official duties, and even so the shop was closed more nights than it was open because of the heavy demands on my time. All this, at a time in life when many people are nearing retirement.

Financially it would be a costly campaign and, as always, there was no "big money" behind me. It would require that I go into debt, and it is a political fact of life that fund-raising efforts are made for the winner, not the losers.

There were innumerable reasons *not* to run, but there were already men in the 1974 race whose records, when compared to their campaign promises, indicated that Georgians were once more being led down the primrose path. I did not feel that I could stand by and let this happen without a fight, and so, at the conclusion of the legislative session in February, I announced that I was a candidate for the Democratic nomination for governor.

It was a crowded field, a situation that always brings up the possibility of a runoff between the top two should no candidate receive a majority. I was the only candidate who was considered as a possible winner without a runoff, and if it did go into a runoff, three of the remaining candidates stood a good chance of being in it. There was David Gambrell, a wealthy Atlanta lawyer who had been Governor Carter's campaign manager in 1970, and who was subsequently appointed by Carter to the United States Senate upon the death of Georgia's venerable and beloved senior senator, Richard B. Russell. Mr. Gambrell, incidentally, under the stigma of being a Carter appointee, was soundly defeated in his effort to be elected to that office in 1972.

There was Bert Lance, a banker from Calhoun, in North Georgia, and another Carter appointee, occupying the chairmanship of the State Highway Department before resigning to enter the governor's race.

Finally, there was State Representative George Busbee, an eighteen-year veteran of the House from Albany, who, despite his disclaimers, had been one of the prime movers behind the controversial Salary Bill discussed in the previous chapter.

My real opposition, however, was not the individuals who were running against me. It was—and always has been—the entrenched power structure, the political establishment, the kingmakers. By whatever name, it is comprised of the leadership of both the Democratic and Republican parties of the state, the leadership—but *not* the rank and file—of labor, the Georgia Association of Educators, the major banks and corporations, the leaders of the black community, and most, if not all, elected state officials who find it more to their own personal, selfish interests to bow down to the political power structure than to stand up like men and fight for the people they supposedly represent. And last, but far from least, the liberal radical media, most notably exemplified by the Cox monopoly—the Atlanta *Journal* and the Atlanta *Constitution*.

For eight years this force had failed to bring Lester Maddox into the fold which seeks to control government by, for, and of the special interest groups. They were afraid because they knew from experience that were I to become governor again they would be in for four more years of the same, that I would never go along with their deals and sinister efforts to subvert the true purpose of the state's government to their benefit and to the detriment of the good, producing citizen-taxpayers to whom it rightly belongs.

I predicted that this campaign would be the ugliest, the most dishonest, meanest, and most expensive I had ever been involved in, and my prediction, unfortunately, became reality. Unable to find any real issue upon which to assault me, they dredged up lies from the past. The Salary Bill, which the Atlanta Newspapers had continued to nurture and keep alive, was brought back full force, and just as before, Lester Maddox was falsely blamed for its passage. Mr. Busbee, who had introduced the bill in the House and had worked assiduously for over two years to get it passed, crisscrossed Georgia declaring that he had *opposed* the bill, and that Lester Maddox was the culprit.

Another charge made against me was that I had not told the truth about my worth and holdings and that I was using cost prices rather than inflated prices. This was a deliberate falsehood, for the appraised value of my holdings in 1974 was *less* than in 1964. When I left office in January 1975, had I disposed of everything I owned I would have realized far less than needed to satisfy my debts. So, in truth, while most business leaders and public officials made their greatest gains in that ten-year period, Lester Maddox was losing.

It is my judgment that these lies—and especially the lie about the Salary Bill—told by my opponents, other cowardly politicians fearful of seeing their own guilt come to light, and poured out endlessly by the liberal-radical news media, are just as shameful, disgraceful, and harmful to political campaigning and good government as anything that occurred in scandalous Watergate.

As the August 13 primary drew near, various polls began to indicate that the sheer weight of the anti-Maddox propaganda was taking hold. I had—realistically, I think—felt early in the campaign that I might win without a runoff. By midsummer, however, it became questionable that I would obtain the required majority of the vote, split as it was among a large field. Of the three top challengers—Gambrell, Lance, and Busbee—one, Mr. Gambrell, had dropped back considerably. It appeared that should the runoff materialize, it would be between myself and either Mr. Busbee or Mr. Lance.

Vast sums of money were being poured in. Mr. Lance alone revealed expenditures approaching the $1 million mark. In my efforts to keep from being entirely obliterated by the saturation tactics of my opponents I was personally in debt more than $300,000. No longer could the campaign be run out of the back of a station wagon.

In addition to the sums announced by the candidates, as

required under disclosure laws, there was the incalculable thrust provided *against* Lester Maddox by the thousands of man-hours and millions of words spewed out by the liberal media. The real issues of the day which I tried to bring before the people were virtually eclipsed by the smoke screen of hatred directed against me as an individual.

On August 13 the voter turnout was light, with scarcely a third of Georgia's registered voters bothering to go to the polls. I led, as was generally conceded I would do, but by a slimmer percentage than I had hoped for. George Busbee came in second. The runoff between Maddox and Busbee was set for September 3. While the principal thrust of virtually all the candidates prior to the August 13 primary had been against Lester Maddox, there had been some parrying and sniping back and forth between the others. Now, however, with three weeks until the runoff, the political establishment pulled firmly together into the most powerful coalition of the in crowd and special interests in the history of the state, to the best of my knowledge, for the single purpose of discrediting and destroying the political life of one man.

The Atlanta *Constitution,* which had earlier announced its support of Lance, quickly switched to Busbee and intensified its editorial tirades and cartoons maligning Lester Maddox. If a lie is told often enough and convincingly enough, it begins to have the ring of truth to many people. Adolf Hitler proved this in the 1930s. The Maddox-haters were determined to prove it again in 1974. And they succeeded, for not only did George Busbee win the runoff, he won by a landslide, polling some 60 per cent of the vote to my 40 per cent.

This defeat was, of course, a personal one for me. But its implications went much further than the political fate of one man. Ideologically, the outcome of the Georgia Democratic primary was perhaps the most significant of any election held in the nation in 1974. The power structure had triumphed; truth, honesty, and open government had suffered a defeat. Clean political campaigning had been all but buried.

When the results were final a reporter came to me. "Some people are saying your loss means that you and what you believe in represent a bygone era," he said. "Do you have a comment to that?"

"I don't believe it's so," I replied, "for if that is the case America will soon be of a bygone era. Morality will be eclipsed by immorality, private enterprise will soon be replaced by socialism and communism, God by atheism. Rights of private property, as we have known them, will have ended. God forbid that these principles and this faith I hold so dear will in reality become principles and faith of a bygone era."

For many years I had tried to believe that most politicians simply "out-promised" themselves when running for office, and were not, for the most part, deliberately lying and misleading the people. This belief was difficult to hang onto, and the gubernatorial campaigns of 1970 and 1974 convinced me once and for all that truth, ethics, and morality do not stand as obstacles in the political paths of many men. I see no escape from the fact that if a candidate for public office is dishonest and untrue in presenting himself and his platform to the people, and he is elected, then he will be a dishonest and lying public official.

From 1970 through 1974 I saw—and tried to stop—political "deals" which were such flagrant examples of this sort of dishonesty as to be almost unbelievable. The so-called "reorganization" of the state government which was glowingly portrayed by the Carter administration as being a panacea for the problems of the people and their government, was, in truth, nothing of the sort. The cost of government skyrocketed. Bureaucracy spread like a cancer. Three times as many jobs paying $20,000 and over were created under reorganization and the Carter administration than in all the previous history of the state's government. State networks, or sub-governments spread across the state, and these became political arms of the in crowd which were used flagrantly, at taxpayers' expense, to carry out campaigns for the establishment's handpicked candidates in the 1974 election.

A particularly odorous piece of special interest legislation was passed by the House and Senate, and signed into law by Governor Carter in 1972. This was a special retirement bill, drawn up by the state Law Department, and in order to cover up its being an administration bill, was introduced in the Senate by a member who was not outwardly identified as being on the Carter "team."

This outright assault on the public treasury provided that if cer-

31. Campaign '74.

32. The Fourth of July Parade, 1974, on Peachtree Street in Atlanta. (Photo by Bob Simms)

33. Relaxing on the verandah of the governor's mansion with Virginia and our basset hound, Pickrick.

34. Producer-director Dan Curtis gives me some stage directions before we begin shooting the first scenes of *The Kansas City Massacre,* an ABC-TV movie, in March 1975. In the film I play the role of governor of Oklahoma during the 1930s. (Photo courtesy Wide World Photos)

tain judges of the Appellate Court retired *before* July 1, 1972, their annual retirement benefit would be $24,000. However, if they were to stay on the bench *beyond* that deadline they would be eligible for exactly half that amount, or $12,000. The obvious purpose of such reverse logic was to create vacancies in choice state jobs in order that the governor might fill them with his political friends and campaign workers.

I have no objection to any governor appointing whomever he sees fit to an appointive state job, if the individual is qualified for the job. I do object vehemently to the use of millions in tax dollars for the sole purpose of creating vacancies in order that the governor might reward his political buddies. This is special interest government of the worst sort, the stealing of tax dollars to bribe officeholders to step aside—*not* to improve the court, but to build the political influence of the governor.

I believe any man, including Lester Maddox, upon being told that he would receive a pension of $24,000 a year if he retired by a given date, and only half that amount if he stayed on, would retire. The distinguished, able, and honorable judges holding the positions resigned as expected.

Special interest legislation, in still another instance, rewards the favored few at the taxpayers' expense. There is no justification, in my judgment, for a man to serve in a part-time elective office for fifteen to twenty years, putting into a retirement fund some $4,000 to $5,000, and then serve as little as four years in high elective or appointive office and qualify for hundreds of thousands of dollars in retirement benefits. Yet this is the case in Georgia, where a man can serve fifteen to twenty years as a legislator—a part-time job—and then serve four years as governor and collect over half a million dollars in the first twenty years of his retirement from that office. (For the record, my eight years as governor and lieutenant governor did not entitle me to retirement benefits.)

This sort of "deal making" in our state government must be stopped. If such dishonesty and cover-up are practiced during the next four years as they have been during the past four, and as they were in the 1970 and 1974 campaigns for the governorship of Georgia, we may well end up with the most dishonest and inefficient government of any of the fifty states. God forbid that this be our fate.

The 1973 Ad Valorem Tax Rebate Bill was yet another example of special interest legislation, in which an across-the-board rebate, as it was originally passed in the House, would have been given in the form of whole chickens to the big shots and chicken feed to the little shots. Thirty-seven million would have gone to the utilities and commercial and industrial property owners, while only $13 million would have been rebated to homeowners and farmers claiming homestead exemption. The bill was sponsored by George Busbee, who, throughout the gubernatorial campaign of 1974, unceasingly proclaimed his concern for the interests of the people.

I complained to then Representative Busbee, to the Speaker of the House, and others of the unfairness of the measure, of how it rewarded the super-rich and cheated the homeowners and farmers, and urged that the formula be reversed. Mr. Busbee replied, in no uncertain terms, that no such change would ever take place. Negotiations came to a halt and the tax relief for homeowners appeared to have been cast aside.

Then something happened that caused Mr. Busbee and others to take pause. The controversial Salary Bill, deadlocked for over two years, passed the Senate. In an effort to take the spotlight off this, the Ad Valorem Tax Rebate Bill was quickly turned around and passed, ultimately giving some $32 million rather than the original proposal of some $13 million in rebates to homeowners and farmers claiming homestead exemption, and about $18 million—or half the original proposal—to the utilities and industrial and commercial property owners.

If the Salary Bill, originally introduced in the House by Mr. Busbee and others, had not finally passed the Senate and House through the combined efforts of Governor Carter, his floor leadership, Representative Busbee and other House leaders, and state officials throughout Georgia, the $50 million Ad Valorem Tax Rebate Bill would never have become law.

And when they found this scheme to take the heat off the salary increases did not work, they looked around for a scapegoat and pinned the tail on Lester Maddox.

As sickening as it is to see professional politicians entrenching themselves in the political establishment through the use—or more correctly the *abuse*—of taxpayers' money, I do not mean this to be a blanket indictment of all elected officials. Most men go into government with high ideals and put far more into government than they get out of it. But it is a sad fact that if a man does not go along with the establishment, if he does not become "one of the boys," he finds his effectiveness weakening, and if he persists in sticking by his guns, pressures are brought to bear which can and will ultimately squeeze him out.

Thus it is almost impossible for a man to remain in high public office for most of his lifetime without becoming a puppet, to one degree or another, of the political establishment. He is then no longer his own man. He is the stereotype of the professional politician, the hack who is governed by politics and fear, and not by what is right.

Of all the frustrations and disappointments in my life none ever compared to those which came my way because of government service. I saw many good men lose their true identity and become tools of the power structure. I never saw a man come out of government more honest than he went in, but I have seen the opposite all too often. It is, without a doubt, a great moral and personal victory for a man to serve in public office and at the same time maintain his honesty and integrity. He must work, pray, and strive in every way to keep from following the easy path. The pressures all about him are tremendous. I have seen them, I have been exposed to them, and I have successfully resisted them.

There is no doubt in my mind that had I been willing to pay the price I could have received the Democratic nomination in 1974 and gone on to become governor of Georgia. The price was too high. To me there is no public office so valuable as to make a man put aside his principles. I have never sought office by deceiving, misleading, or lying to the people, nor have I ever considered becoming a puppet of the political establishment. They knew this, and as a result the 1974 campaign never became one of truth, or who might be the best man, who had the best platform, or what might be in the best interest of the people of Georgia.

The issue, as planned for years by the political establishment, including Governor Carter and the Atlanta Newspapers, was to rid the state's government of Lester Maddox regardless of what lies had to be told, or what truths had to be covered up, or of the cost to the people and to good government. The results of the 1974 elections, and of 1970 as well, lend strong credence to those who feel we may have reached the point in politics where the candidates attempting to tell the truth are least likely to be elected, while those who lie, cover up, and deceive the most are the likeliest to gain office.

It was evident on August 13 and again on September 3 that hundreds of thousands of Georgians had come to believe the lie connecting Lester Maddox to the infamous Salary Bill. Those who propagated it—Jimmy Carter, George Busbee, and scores of others who were trying to cover up their own guilt by placing the blame on the only state official who fought the bill from beginning to end—performed a grave injustice, not only to a guiltless man, but to the people of Georgia.

It is my fervent hope and prayer that each man's conscience will leave him shamed and restless for this wrong until he comes forward and makes a clean breast of it. The people of Georgia deserve to know the truth, not only from the power-mad and dishonest politicians who deliberately lied to them but also from the dishonest media. And not only should the people hear the truth from these but they should hear it from the scores of other state officials who *know* that Lester Maddox fought the salary increase bill and *know* those who are guilty of its passage. May that day finally come when they will muster the courage, integrity, and truth to be fair, open, and honest.

I am convinced that there will be no significant cleanup in our government until there is a cleanup in campaigning for elective office. And there will be no cleanup in this area until a way is found to punish those who deliberately lie and intentionally mislead the voters. Our present campaign disclosure laws will never accomplish what is needed; they merely swat at gnats while elephants pass freely, and the elephants grow larger with each year.

All too often it is the candidate who has lied and deceived the most who wins the race, and in far too many cases he is the man who has the blessing and support of the political establishment, and the endorsement of the liberal, and often unfair and dishonest, news media.

Candidates and public officials have been felled by assassins' bullets, but far fewer have gone down in this manner than the number destroyed or crippled by the dishonest campaigns directed against them or by the poisoned, unfair, and dishonest pens and voices of the news media.

Chapter 13

Stand Up for America

Few men have more reason than I to say "amen" to Harry Truman's admonition to get out of the kitchen if you can't stand the heat. Through four years as governor of Georgia, and another four as lieutenant governor I took the brunt of more unfair criticism and biased reporting than any other five men who have held either of those offices. I was called racist, when in fact far more opportunities were opened to black people in state government than under all previous administrations. When I held the line against irresponsible and unbridled spending of taxpayers' money by MARTA, I was labeled "anti-rapid transit." A "back-door" salary increase was finally rammed through the legislature and signed into law by Governor Jimmy Carter, and the man they tried to blame for it was the man who had fought it steadfastly for three years: Lester Maddox. During the highly volatile days following the shooting of Martin Luther King I took quiet but firm steps as governor to protect the property and the lives of the citizens of Atlanta and Georgia while cities all over America were in flames, and I was called "little," and was said to be "cowering in the Capitol." I was even accused of undignified conduct as governor because I was photographed riding a bicycle backwards on the mansion drive. The list is endless.

Hot as the Pickrick kitchens got, they never came close to the heat of the Capitol. But I learned long ago that the only time the kitchen got cool was when it was closed for business, and there was—and is—too much to be done to spend time swatting at the flies whose stock in trade is innuendo and untruth.

The survival of this country is continually at stake, and if it is to survive as a free republic, if sensible and constitutional government is to be restored and preserved, it will not be because of those sitting on the sidelines shouting insults, rather it will be accomplished by God-fearing men and women who are not afraid to take positive action, and who are not deterred simply because the kitchen has gotten hot.

I am an optimist. Even when those closest to me had given up all hope that my campaign for the governorship of Georgia in 1966 would be successful, I never doubted for one minute that my destiny was to serve Georgians in the state's highest office. I never prayed that God would get me elected, but then, as now, my prayer was that God would use me as He saw fit and to give me the wisdom and strength to be a true and honest man.

I had to be an optimist, for after a few weeks in office I had seen enough to discourage any man. I saw state employees working half a day for a full day's wages. I saw prisons unfit for human habitation. High state officials were found to be involved in questionable practices. Schoolteachers were discontented and many were moving on to teach in other states or to move into other professions or into business. Crime was rampant, and some local law enforcement officials were believed to be collaborating with the criminals —or how else could crime flourish under their very eyes?

I had cooked an awful lot of chicken in my life, but this was my first experience dealing with a buzzard. So, not knowing any better, I just picked the whole thing up by the tail and let the feathers fly where they would. My method caused quite a stink at first. Some people said I was not being loyal to the party, and some said I was carrying on a witch hunt and stirring up trouble just for publicity. But we got the job started, and the idea caught on. People began to talk about topics that were not too popular to talk about. Some of the old hogs at the state trough went looking for a handout elsewhere. Changes began to take place. Slowly, the government of the state was coming back into the hands of the people, where it belonged.

I have always subscribed to the Jeffersonian concept that local self-government is the best government, that people do a far better job of solving their problems at the local level with an absolute minimum of interference from big government. America, unfortunately, has been going in the opposite direction in the grip of one liberal national administration after another, Democrat and Republican alike. The old virtues of self-reliance, free enterprise, and self-sufficiency have faded in today's tilted sense of values. If it is old-fashioned to remind ourselves of the solidity and good sense that are the heritage of America, then I am old-fashioned.

I am so old-fashioned that I believe children should mind their parents instead of parents minding their children.

I am so old-fashioned that I believe every able man should earn his own way and determine his own destiny according to his ambitions and efforts.

I am so old-fashioned that I am proud to love my country and its flag, and regard defending both as a privilege and duty.

I am so old-fashioned that I believe God is alive and that He made man in His own image and gave him the holy responsibility to be his brother's keeper.

I am so old-fashioned that I believe, as Abraham Lincoln did, that

". . . you cannot strengthen the weak by weakening the strong . . .

". . . you cannot help small men by tearing down big men . . .

". . . you cannot help the poor by destroying the rich . . .

". . . you cannot lift the wage-earner by pulling down the wage payer . . .

". . . you cannot keep out of trouble by spending more than you make . . .

". . . you cannot further the brotherhood of man by inciting class hatreds."

This great country of ours did not just happen. The early settlers knew that the only way for a nation to be exalted was through submission to the Lord. They knew that America could not be great unless it was good, and they knew full well that they could not be good without God. This country was blessed because our forefathers publicly and unashamedly sought to follow God's statutes and prayed for wisdom and direction from Him. The father of our country, George Washington, said, "No nation can rightly be governed without God and the Bible."

The spiritual wealth of our people has seen us through one crisis after another—the Revolutionary War, Civil War, World War I, the Great Depression of the 1930s, and World War II. Since that war, America has placed great emphasis on meeting the material needs of the people, and there is no question but what these needs are great. But in our zeal to fulfill our material needs we have neglected to put proper emphasis on human and spiritual needs.

This preoccupation with materialism has sown the seeds of moral decay and this has flourished to such an extent that the greatest poverty in America is not of dollars and material things. It is a spiritual poverty. A poverty in the lives of church people who have left the fellowship of the Lord's house and who are living in the wasteland of sin. It is a poverty of courage among parents who know that government is moving to control and ruin education in this country, but who fail to speak against it or do anything about it for fear of being criticized.

There is a poverty of honest concern on the part of many people for the fate of the children of America and the fate of the country's future as these people become so occupied with business and pleasure that they make the mistake of entrusting high political office year after year to bleeding-heart liberals, never stopping to consider that these men support programs and philosophies which are undermining the very foundations of our free society.

Unless there is a reversal of this trend toward complete control over our children, our schools, our businesses, our lives by the federal government, we are inevitably headed toward that day when our nation will cease to be a free republic.

Dwight D. Eisenhower said in 1950: "I firmly believe that the army of persons who urge greater and greater centralization of authority and greater and greater dependence upon the Federal treasury are really more dangerous than any external threat."

I sometimes wonder what George Washington, Thomas Jefferson, Andrew Jackson, and other great Americans of the past would say if they were alive today. These men who fought to create and preserve the freedoms that are the foundation of this country would be shocked to see the war being waged upon law enforcement, private enterprise, public education, the rights of property and morality, and they would be doubly shocked to see that this war is being waged and encouraged by the federal government they themselves created.

They would surely see the parallel in history. In the fifth century the Roman Empire was a world leader. The Roman economy had never been better, her interest spanned the known world, her armies were feared and respected. But because of a loss of spiritual direction, a crisis in government, and inward moral decay, Rome was destroyed.

The Huns and the Vandals came from the North and ravaged Rome. But it had not been the enemy from without who had brought Rome down, it had been the decay from within.

The great tragedy of our time is that countless thousands of misled Americans have been brainwashed by those who are playing the game of being god and have surrendered their freedoms, their integrity, individualism, their faith, and sometimes their very soul in order to get more money, more votes, and more material security. The Watergate tragedy is symptomatic of this, the apparent result of men thinking that, because of their rank or position in society, they can write their own rules and appeal to a higher law within the confines of their own political citadel. God warns us: "Whatsoever a man soweth that shall he also reap." In the Watergate we have seen men sow to the wind, and now they are reaping a whirlwind of distrust and confusion.

The prospect of discovering another America is very remote, and unless we win the victory over the forces of atheism and tyranny in our time, we will have lost the world's last free republic.

Where is the Answer? God. The Holy Bible. With God, America will prosper in peace. Without God, America will perish. It is as simple as that. It is so obvious to me that I simply cannot understand why others in and out of public office cannot see it.

When I closed my business because our government had so eroded the freedoms our founding fathers had tried to guarantee us that I no longer had the freedom to operate my own business as I saw fit, I erected a memorial to those lost freedoms, and I wrote an epitaph. More than a decade later, sadly, that epitaph is even more appropriate than it was then. This is what I wrote:

EPITAPH TO THE WORLD'S GREATEST
FREE REPUBLIC

As long as I live and breathe, I will continue to fight
for the preservation of the United States of America as a

free republic. But if I should lose in my battle, and our great nation ultimately is lost to the enemies of God, the enemies of freedom, and the enemies of the American way of life, I hope someone at least will build a memorial to the greatest nation the world has ever known. And on this memorial, I would propose that we engrave the following epitaph:

Here lies the remains of the United Sates of America, born a free republic on July 4, 1776, in Philadelphia, Pennsylvania, delivered by the hands of patriots who so loved freedom that they dared to demand it, standing ready to sacrifice their fortunes, and even their very lives, to insure that freedom was established and preserved.

The infant republic was threatened from every quarter. Its own mother country sought to end its life with the sword. Hostile forces, coming by ship and by horseback, tortured the infant with cannon, arrow, and pen, but the infant continued to survive and grow and prosper, nurtured by the love of men and women, now long forgotten, who would not accept tyranny at any price.

And the young nation grew to adolescence. In this period of its growth, it was torn in half by divergent philosophies. Weak from loss of blood, the wounds healed slowly. But, nourished by a strong faith in God and the principles of private enterprise, private property rights, states' rights, and respect for human dignity, the scars of civil war all but completely faded, and the century-old nation matured to become a giant among nations.

Many were envious of the wealth and prosperity of the relatively young republic. While Americans sang songs about "spacious skies," "amber waves of grain," and "fruited plains," nations without America's degree of freedom cried out for food to feed their starving and flocked to the shores of the one nation which promised every individual an opportunity to reach his full potential.

The greedy came not with outstretched hands, but with clenched fists. But America, with unprecedented indus-

trial muscles developed through the system of private enterprise, and with an unyielding spirit born of a long life
of freedom, turned back every aggressor and remained
the greatest nation of all time.

But, then, with a full belly, weary of war and confident
that the land and the hard-won freedom was secure, the
giant went to sleep. The American people became apathetic. They stored away their feelings of patriotism along
with the flags they once waved so proudly. Politicians
became followers rather than leaders, and, as crime swept
the nation, government failed in its first responsibility,
that of protecting the lives and properties of its citizens.
The people ceased to be secure in their homes and safe
on the streets.

The people surrendered public education, but a million
times more important, they surrendered their children—
America's most precious resource—to a federal "police
state" which acted without constitutional authority in
stealing away the rights and freedoms of America's
children and their parents.

America turned from God, grew self-righteous and began playing God rather than praying to Him as communism, drug addiction, pornography and immorality ate
away the moral and spiritual strength of the nation.

When tyrants came to the giant, nudged him with riots,
anarchy, crime, wars and threats of wars, the giant just
mumbled an "okay," rather than wake up and fight.

And so, gradually, communism and socialism replaced
capitalism and freedom. Private property rights were
abolished a little at a time. The U. S. Constitution was re-
written by judicial tyrants and bureaucratic dictators until
it became totally meaningless and was discarded.

Human dignity and personal initiative were gradually
eroded and replaced with government handout programs
until, finally, everybody was getting a government
paycheck and there was nobody working to produce the
needed wealth.

Faith in God was replaced by faith in man, faith in

government, faith in political parties, and faith in the immortality of the United States of America.

In his last moments, the giant opened his eyes. In a last valiant effort, he tried to get to his feet, but he was kicked back down by the iron boot of tyranny.

His last words were, "Don't give up hope. All we need is more dollars . . . just a few more dollars . . . just a few more dollars."

May the greatest nation the world has ever known rest in peace.

God forbid that this be the fate of America. If it is to be otherwise, we cannot depend upon the selfish politician, the atheist, the anarchist, the communist, the welfare stater or the coward.

If the epitaph I have described for America is to be avoided, then it will be through the efforts of real statesmen, those who believe in and love God enough to live so, those who build and produce, the defenders of private enterprise and Americanism, those who put America first, and those who are courageous.

In order to put us back on the right path, I would begin with an open letter to the President of the United States and to the Congress:

Why, Mr. President and Members of Congress, do you not lead a fight to set aside the United States Supreme Court ruling which made it illegal for America's boys and girls to be led in prayer and Bible reading in our public schools?

It is legal, gentlemen, for you and other Americans to be led in prayer and Bible reading in the White House, the Congress, the courts, the statehouses, and the city halls. You and other Americans can be led in prayer and Bible reading on the public streets, at sporting events, and at social, civic, business, and patriotic gatherings throughout America. Yet how tragic it is that the only place in our great country where our government rules it illegal to be led in prayer and Bible reading is in our public schools.

Knowing that it continues to be legal for students to be

taught atheism, socialism, communism, and evolution in our public schools we must remove the ban which makes it illegal for them to be led in prayer and Bible reading in these same public schools.

Please, Mr. President and Congressmen, I beg you to help right this wrong. For the sake of our youth, our country, and freedom, you must not do less, for in doing less you will fail America and her children.

I believe that your most fervent desire, like mine, is to make certain that the United States of America survives as a free republic and that freedom shall never vanish from our shores. But I am convinced that unless you have the courage and patriotism to change from the present course of government which is failing America, our freedom and our republic will be lost.

The enemies of God and America have boasted that communism would bury us and that our grandchildren would live under communism. It is terrifying to see that their boast has been turning toward reality with little resistance and much encouragement and assistance, planned or not, by our own government.

A war is being waged in this country upon law enforcement, private enterprise, public education, the rights to private property, and morality. Your duty as America's leaders demands that you join the war against these forces and go all out for America . . . even if it means losing the next election. The fate of America is in your hands. May God give you the courage to accept the challenge.

However, the President and the Congress cannot do what needs to be done alone. I would direct another plea to the people of this nation:

My dear fellow Americans, contrary to what too many people think, our national government does not belong just to the "in crowd," nor only to the Democrats or the Republicans, the black, the white, the weak, the strong, nor to any special interest group. And although we are witnessing destructive and threatening encroachments upon our rights and freedoms we can thank God that the criminals, the communists, the mistaken, the anarchists, and the self-serving politicians have not yet taken over our government.

The truth, my fellow citizens, is that this great land belongs to *all* Americans. Yet the sad fact is that far too many of us who work for a living, who love God, and who are loyal to our country are not claiming our share of America and protecting it.

Most productive Americans are careful, as indeed they should be, in how they spend their money for food, clothing, housing, transportation, and other necessities and luxuries. Yet these hard-working and productive citizens will put more of their earnings into the combined levels of government, where their freedom will either live or die, than into the combined expenditure for food, clothing, housing, and transportation during their lifetimes, and far too many Americans are leaving their government and their tax dollars to the destroyers. This apathy and indifference about what is done with their tax dollars must end, or our freedom as a people and our form of government as a free republic will soon end.

It is a sad fact that most politicians, regardless of their good intentions, become followers rather than leaders. Their decisions in too many instances result from political pressure rather than from what may be right, and for far too long the pressure has been coming from the socialist, the communist, the bum, the criminal, and the special interest groups.

Your duty and mine, my fellow Americans, is clear. The destructive course we presently follow must be reversed. This land is *your* land. The United States Government belongs to you, and I am pleading with you to get involved in your government and speak out and stand up for God and America as never before.

Regardless of what many would have us believe, it was not just great presidents, great congressmen, great governors, and great judges who made America the bastion of freedom it has been. What really made this country great and free was its being blessed by God because our forefathers publicly and unashamedly sought to follow His statutes. We were blessed with men like George Washington, who said, "No nation can rightly be governed without God and the Bible"; Nathan Hale, who proudly and courageously gave his life rather than betray his country; Daniel Webster, who said, "God grants liberty only to those who love it and stand ready to guard and defend it"; and Ben Franklin, who called our forefathers into prayer to seek God's wisdom at a time when it appeared they would be unable to complete the Constitution.

If the United States is to survive, it will not be because of politicians who campaign on one platform and then live by another. It will not be because of the actions of the do-gooders, the bleeding hearts, the hypocrites, the welfare staters, the one-worlders, or those millions of apathetic Americans who do little or nothing for their country and who prefer to leave to others the job of fighting to maintain freedom.

If America is to survive, it will take more honest and courageous candidates for public office, more officeholders who would rather be right than be elected, and more Americans in and out of government whose faith in God and love for freedom, America, and truth is of sufficient strength for them to speak out for, and live by, their principles.

To the youth of America, who have more at stake in this country than any of us, I would say, do not get turned on to drugs. Get turned on for God and stay turned on for Him. And do not get hooked on the crazy idea that the world owes you a living, that socialism and communism are good, and that working for a living, believing in private enterprise, and having faith in God are taboo.

Whatever you do, do not fall victim to those teachings that downgrade God, private enterprise, capitalism, private property rights, and our constitutional government. These are the ingredients that made America great and free.

Have no truck with the dishonesty and hypocrisy you see daily all around you, but be honest and true with yourself, your fellow-man, your country, and your God. America's future belongs to your generation, not mine. Do these things better than my generation has done them and you will leave America a better, safer, cleaner, and freer place than the America my generation is passing on to you. My prayer is that you not fail, for if you fail, so will America.

INDEX